Wh
Ma.

MW01169903

"I really enjoyed this book. Being both a dog owner and managing a team of people, I can truly relate to the situations presented. I thought the book was an easy read with straight forward solutions to everyday problems that occur, in both the workplace as well as the canine world. Strong communication skills is one of the most important attributes to being a respected & highly effective team manager…and the same holds true in training a well-behaved dog."

Scott Wisman, CRPC®, CIMA®, CPFA® | Managing Director | Wealth Management Advisor Wisman / Willis / Moran Group Merrill; Lynch, Pierce, Fenner & Smith Inc.

"A fun yet practical read with important leadership strategies shared through the lens of a dog-loving owner and accomplished professional."

George Hanson, Vice President, North America E-Commerce and Retail, Under Armour, Inc.

"While this book is titled Management Unleashed, it's more of a leadership lesson and truly hits home on so many points we'd never consider in our daily lives. Many times we overlook the simple lessons; this book delivers just that in showing how simply training your dog can carry over into life lessons on leadership, taking control, confidence, teaching, and managing people to accomplish a common goal. It was enjoyable and a book that was hard to put down as you want to keep reading since it's very easy to see your daily life represented by the characters within the story."

Steve Montgomery, Owner of The Starboard Restaurant

"With all the books on the market today that focus on the latest and greatest management theory, it's refreshing to find one that brings us back to what makes a successful manager. Management Unleashed shows, in an engaging way, how some of the practices used to train our dogs are based on the same principles that make for successful managers. An easy and eye-opening read that is valuable for new and experienced managers alike."

G.M. (Bud) Benscoter, PhD; Owner, GMB Performance Group

"I really enjoyed the concept of this book! Not only is it a fun read, but it contains very helpful information for dog owners and managers alike."

Sarah Curtis, DVM; Rehoboth Beach Animal Hospital; Rehoboth Beach, DE

"Hanson and Cameron have creatively adapted an array of canine learnings to effective organizational management."

M. William (Bill) Lower; Vice President—Environmental & Governmental Affairs; Harvey Hanna & Associates, Inc.

"This book makes a difficult reality, managing coworkers through a deadline, more bite-size by relating it to more familiar territory, such as navigating relationships with friends or pets. I learned that the same practices that make someone a faithful friend or a caring pet owner—actively listening, regularly investing time, and clearly communicating expectations—are the same qualities that lay the foundation for effective leadership."

Laura Barton, Esq.; Goldstein & Associates, LLC

MANAGEMENT UNLEASHED

Leadership Lessons From My Dog

DIANE HANSON · TODD CAMERON

Copyright ©2018 Diane Hanson and Todd Cameron

Cover Design by Crystal Heidel

Paw print, artwork by FreeVector.com

ISBN-13: 978-1729800508

ISBN-10: 1729800505

Second Edition

Published by Sandy Paws Press

Printed in the United States of America

Dedication

To my mother and husband
Diane

To Sharon and my girls
Todd

Contents

Acknowledgements

It is with gratitude that I thank the many people who helped write and publish this book.

Co-author Todd Cameron offered creativity and added humor to the manuscript. Without his assistance, the book may never have been completed.

Maribeth Fisher, Executive Director of the Rehoboth Writer's Guild, along with encouragement, offered opportunities to improve my writing and to get this book published.

Ginny Downie provided excellent suggestions and edits along with additional encouragement through her genuine enthusiasm for the book.

Dog trainer, Mary Hughes, helped me see the light in terms of the connections between dog and human behavior.

A special thank you goes to all the reviewers—too numerous to mention individually—who read the book and offered suggestions and edits.

This book was a product of decades of work, review and editing and there are many people who helped along the way. I am thankful to all of you.
—Diane Hanson

I want to thank my collaborator, Diane Hanson, whose extraordinary talent for making great things happen brought this book to life from an initial conversation on Dewey Beach many years ago.

Also, kudos to Laura Barton, whose insights made this a better book. Finally, a monumentous thank you to the love of my life and all-time favorite, Sharon, who moved mountains so I could help create this.
—Todd Cameron

Chapter 1

Can You Really Teach an Old Dog New Tricks?

I was in over my head. The Kramer Franton Inc. account was in a death spiral. Up against an impossible deadline, my team was falling apart. If things didn't turn around quickly, people were going to lose their jobs. Kramer and Frantic, as we affectionately called it, is a manufacturing company looking to improve efficiency with our latest software. I had inherited the account with my new assignment less than two months ago, and my company was making haste to get it done.

To say the meeting with our client went poorly is an understatement. In fact, it was nothing short of a miracle that KFI was still our client.

Rain pelted my windshield, outpacing my wipers. As I accelerated back toward the office for my meeting, I cranked up the radio and switched the wipers to high speed.

Friday meetings that begin at 4:00 rarely conclude with, "Have a nice weekend." This was no exception. Coming out of that meeting, I knew Nate was back in the office because an ominous quiet had swept across row upon row of still-occupied cubicles. There was no animated talk of happy hour or weekend plans, just an orchestra of keyboards clacking away. *Damn, I thought Nate was supposed to be out all day.*

Back in my office, I was relieved to see no new texts or voicemail. The last thing I wanted to think about on my wedding anniversary weekend was the fragile KFI account.

Hoping to get a jumpstart to the beach for the weekend, I started tidying up. But as I tucked a recent snapshot of our new dog, Dewey, into the bottom corner of a framed portrait of Hank and me in our golf gear in Bermuda, I suddenly heard the dreaded beep of a text. The unwelcome text read, "See me ASAP—N." My heart sank, and something in my gut told me I wasn't getting out of here anytime soon.

Nate's corner office was at the end of a long corridor flanked by recently vacated offices of former execs that had left the company suddenly under undisclosed circumstances. I stuck my head into the slightly open door, knocking faintly. Typing furiously, he was speaking into a phone cradled along his neck. Making eye contact, he circled his hand in the air, summoning me. Everyone else was in khakis on "casual Friday," but not Nate; he used to be all pinstripes and wingtips but he traded them in for country club casual. An alpha-dog wannabe, he would have worn the same thing even if he weren't meeting with a client.

"Yes, yes," he nodded into the phone. "That will be all." He hung up, rubbed a manicured hand through his anchorman power haircut, and turned to me. "Marti, I just got back from our friends at Kramer, and they're not happy."

I suppressed the urge to say, "That's an understatement."

As Nate launched into an update on the situation, all I could think about was Hank back at home, loading his golf clubs into the car, looking forward to a relaxing weekend at the beach.

Nate's phone rang. Looking at the caller ID, he said, "I'm sorry—I have to take this. I'll just be a sec."

Ten minutes into that sec, sitting as patiently as I could, listening to half a conversation with apparently no end in sight, I glanced out the window at the rapidly-emptying parking lot. I could see my lonely tan Accord baking in the late afternoon sun now that the rain had ceased. Mercifully, I heard Nate utter an insincere, "Have a nice weekend," as he put down the receiver. He muttered a quick apology and continued, "We need to get the Kramer implementation back on track. They've given us a timeframe."

"How long?"

"I asked for three months. They're giving us half that."

"Six weeks?" I gasped in awkward response and suddenly felt a headache coming on strong as Nate nodded.

"Marti, I realize that you haven't been with our division for very long." It was true. Although I had been here at Prism Consulting for five years, I had only recently moved into the Large Accounts Division. I was just getting the feel for this place, getting to know my team.

He continued, "Money is tight. I can't increase your budget or add resources to this, but Kramer still needs the Omega e-Business Suite Software up and running in six weeks. I want a revised project plan by end of business Wednesday."

"But, Nate, we've never completed a software implementation in that short a timeframe, even for the smaller companies in the Middle Market Group."

"Well, you're in a new group now and you'll have to think bigger and smarter." Apparently, logical rules didn't apply, I mused.

"After two bad quarters in a row, we can't afford a third. If we lose Kramer, I don't have to tell you the consequences." Nate paused and asked, "Can you get the team together for a minute?"

"Right now?"

Nate was oblivious to the fact that people generally didn't like to work late on Fridays, especially in the summer. The mass exodus had probably begun the moment I closed Nate's door.

"Why not?"

"Most of the team has already left for the weekend. Besides, I'd like to plan a little first."

"Then you'll brief the team first thing Monday morning and come up with an implementation training plan?"

I nodded. I would have to work like a dog to get ready for that Monday morning meeting. It looked like my laptop was going to the beach with me.

As I walked out of his office, Nate called to me, "Oh, and by the way, have a nice weekend."

I left text messages for my team about the Monday morning meeting before leaving. I called Hank on the way home to let him know I was running behind. To make matters worse, traffic was at a standstill.

"Hank, I'm sooo sorry. You know how Nate is."

"I cancelled our dinner reservation. The traffic will be ridiculous now." Hank sighed. "I guess we can eat some place around here before we head to the beach. Wait 'til you hear about Dewey's latest escapade!"

"Sure, lay it on me." But the cell phone signal was breaking up. "Hank, I can barely hear you."

"Well, you can see when you get home."

I could tell from his icy tone that the dog's latest adventure was not a good one. I could also tell that Dewey wasn't the only one in the doghouse tonight.

When I finally got home, Dewey was outside, tied to a front porch post. He gave me his usual high-energy greeting, barking excitedly without a shred of guilt and easily jumping twice his height. As I opened the door and looked beyond the foyer, my jaw dropped. It was mid-summer, but it looked like a blizzard had hit our living room. Dewey had eaten the couch! I had searched for that couch for months and waited two more months to have it custom-made. Now, the wooden arms were chewed beyond recognition. Cushion stuffing was everywhere.

Chewy Dewey had struck again.

"All that, and I've already vacuumed twice," Hank said, appearing around the corner with a fresh bag for the Hoover. He was smiling; that meant I was already forgiven for getting home late. Thankfully, it would take more than an indoor blizzard to bring him down.

After a quick kiss, he said, "I've got some good news and some bad news about my teaching schedule."

"Good first."

"The good news is that Higgins decided he doesn't want to teach Shakespeare for the summer term. So I'm in!"

"That's fantastic! You've wanted to teach that class for years."

"Higgins hates summer term. This could mean tenure for me." Hank, a literature professor specializing in Shakespeare, had almost made tenure twice in the past ten years. Teaching this class was too big an opportunity to pass up.

"The bad news is that the class meets Monday nights."

"Uh-huh."

"Starting this Monday."

"Well, that is short notice, but you're prepared. So the problem is?"

"We're signed up for dog training that night."

"We can reschedule."

"No, we can't. Jenna isn't teaching again until late October. Look around you—there's no question that Dewey needs all the training he can get right now. He's chewing us out of house and home. Look at the sofa arms. He must be part cocker spaniel, part poodle, and part termite!"

It's true! Dewey was out of control, and Hank's mother gave us a certificate for dog training that was sorely needed. I could just hear her rant about how much the dog training cost and how Jenna Braddock was the greatest dog trainer in the country and how she actually lived here in town and how people have to get on a class waiting list before their puppies are even born.

"It's only six weeks," Hank added.

Only six weeks, I thought.

"All right, all right. I'll be there." I wasn't sure how. I had to get my work project completed during that same period of time or I might be unemployed soon, I thought, but at least I would have a better-behaved dog.

Chapter 2

Communication: They Have to Know What You Expect

Giving bad or unpopular news is a skill I've never mastered, and I was acutely aware of this as I approached my team on Monday morning shortly before eight. As I walked over to my team's bank of cubicles, I asked, "May I have everyone's attention?" One by one, their chairs swiveled around to face me with all the energy of a pack of bears coming out of hibernation—slowly and heavily.

First out of the cave was our resident pit bull, Kevin Breen, grimacing as if he couldn't be bothered. As he turned his head down to look at his legal pad, I could see that the patch of bare scalp at the back of his head had gotten visibly larger in the past few months. The way the part in his still-black hair flowed into his bald spot made it look like a golf club or musical note. At fifty-five, he was older than the others, but not wiser. He hadn't been promoted in years, but he stayed on because the right people liked him and he knew where all the bodies were buried.

Rapidly typing one final sentence before turning around, Grace Freeman looked up next. Mountains of paper covered her desk, but she always knew where everything was. And although she was a fairly new hire, she was very competent and stayed on top of things.

"Where's Alex?" I asked. Grace and Kevin shook their heads. "Well, let's get started." As I began the meeting, recent grad, Alex Brennan, came running in late, as usual, clutching a jumbo Starbucks cup. His hair was still wet and a couple of weeks overdue for a cut, and his shirt wasn't quite tucked into his pants. Mumbling an apology, he quickly slunk into his chair, trying to look as attentive as possible to avoid drawing further attention.

"As you know, KFI is in the final phase of implementing the Omega 3.0 e-Business Suite. Our group is responsible for the training, end-to-end testing, and change-management initiative. This project is already six months behind schedule."

"It's their fault!" interrupted Kevin, rising from his chair. "They keep changing the requirements." Even standing, Kevin didn't seem much taller than everyone sitting. Waving his arms about, he said, "You can't expect us to provide the deliverables on time under these conditions." For many employees at Prism, complaining was a way of life, yet Kevin had raised it to an art form.

"Kevin, let me finish," I said. "Nate met with Tyler Harding from KFI on Friday. They're not happy campers. They want results soon, and we need to bring this project to a close. I need you all to get together and come up with a plan to wrap up this project right away."

"How soon do you need it?" asked Alex.

"Six weeks."

"That's ridiculous!" Kevin blurted. "This project won't come together that fast. We need more time. This is insane!" He glared at me as he shook his head in disgust.

"Kevin, it's aggressive, but our timeline is no longer negotiable. That's what we need to do if we are going to save this client and Prism's reputation. Undoubtedly, it will take great effort and extra hours to meet their expectations."

My team had no idea how bad things were. They knew only that we were behind schedule. They knew that KFI was not exactly thrilled with us. Did they think KFI would just keep extending our deadline and let us slide? They had seen layoffs in other departments when Prism lost accounts. Were they in denial? Prism was failing and failing fast.

THAT NIGHT, DEWEY DARTED HAPPILY INTO MY CAR, and off to our first class we went. Jenna Braddock's farm sat in the zone where the suburbs ended and small towns began. Locals called it "Doggy Boot Camp." As I pulled into the parking lot, I saw kennels for boarding and corrals for dogs to exercise. The website said that the class was in the barn.

Dewey thrashed his head back and forth in the back seat, as I fastened the leash to his collar. I spotted another woman walking her Great Dane across the gravel parking lot toward the barn. Dewey immediately growled at the gentle giant, straining against his leash and kicking up gravel like a bull about to charge a matador. "Dewey, stop!" I commanded, praying the leash would hold as Dewey lurched forward again. How could a creature so cute sound so ferocious? The Great Dane had every right to floss his teeth with Dewey's fur, but he completely ignored my dog, infuriating Dewey further. All this, and we hadn't even entered the barn yet!

The vestibule inside the refinished barn resembled a dog-training history museum. Its walls were lined with glass display cases filled with dog show trophies, plaques of recognition from the SPCA, and even a plaque from the State Police Academy for excellence in K-9 training.

I moved into the main room which looked a little like a high school gymnasium. Ten other owners were already in a circle, their leashed dogs milling around, sniffing one another. I chose a spot as far from the Great Dane as I could. But Dewey turned back toward the door and started growling again as a gigantic, moppy sheep dog burst into the room, dragging a petite brunette woman behind him, her feet sliding on the slippery wooden floor like a clumsy water skier. "Whoa, Buddy, whoa!" she yelled in vain as Buddy joined the sniffing party.

Suppressing a laugh, I turned to her as she approached. "Look at my dog growling away. He doesn't behave any better, so I guess we're in the right place. By the way, I'm Marti."

"I'm Sue. What's your dog's name?"

"Dewey. I already know Buddy's name."

Soon a little dachshund started barking. Another dog joined in. Then another. Suddenly, all barking stopped as an extremely fit woman in shorts and a polo shirt strode into the room. She was only five feet two, but her spiky black hair and confident posture signaled that she was in charge. She had the sturdy demeanor of a drill sergeant, the ropey arms of a rock climber or yoga expert, and the powerful legs of a gymnast. Everyone knew that this had to be Jenna Braddock.

After brief introductions, Jenna got right to the first lesson: "Effective dog training begins with clear communication. Dogs need us to be specific about what we want. So start by giving clear directions."

Buddy suddenly jumped up on his hind legs, lurching toward Jenna, tail wagging furiously, jerking the leash taut once more. Sue let out an "oomph!" as Buddy nearly pulled her down.

Without breaking her stride, Jenna turned toward Buddy and Sue and continued, "While a dog may appear to be hyperactive, submissive, or defiant, it usually means the dog is unsure about what you want. If your intentions are unclear or your expectations are inconsistent, your dog will go into instant self-gratification mode. In other words, he'll ignore you and do what he wants. When this happens, the dog gets confused, and we get frustrated."

"May I?" Jenna asked as she politely took Buddy's leash from Sue to demonstrate. "First, you must hold the leash properly. Grasp it loosely near your belly with one hand and use your other hand to exert control as needed. She led Buddy through a series of turns, changes of speed, and other quick movements. Buddy followed right along. The instant he went the wrong way or stopped paying attention, she gave him a quick tug (also known as a check) with the leash. Jenna made it look easy as Buddy followed her willingly.

"That's amazing," marveled Sue.

Handing the leash back to Sue, Jenna explained, "Your dog should follow every move with the leash held loosely. When they don't do as they're supposed to, give them a check—a quick, slightly downward, tug on their leash—and they'll fall in line."

My classmates mumbled as if it were impossible.

Jenna turned to Dewey and me. "Now, it's your turn, Marti. Let's see you lead Dewey in a straight line." It sounded easy, but when I tried, Dewey pulled me in the opposite direction with a forceful tug that would have made Buddy proud.

"Whoa!" Jenna exclaimed. "Be very clear about what you want him to do. Don't take no for an answer." She took hold of Dewey's leash, gave it a sharp tug, and off they went. Immediately, Jenna had Dewey's attention, and he followed, eagerly heeling behind her. "If you get into a tugging match with your dog, the dog sees this as a game, and he'll play all day. But that's obviously not what you want. Instead, let him know what you expect with a quick check on his leash that guides him in the right direction. He'll learn to watch you and follow along."

A light bulb went off in my head. I thought of Kevin and our perpetual game of tug-of-war, and decided I would take what I learned from Jenna—and Dewey—to the office.

After others had a chance to practice leading their dogs on a leash and get pointers from Jenna, she concluded our first day of training by adding, "The final thought I'd like to leave you with is that consistency is essential. Every member of the family must use the same words for the same command. All of you must say, DOWN not Lie down or some other words. Dogs don't understand English. They only know the words you teach them. Using several different words and expecting the same result doesn't work. It confuses them."

Jenna smiled at the group as they pondered what she was saying. She wrapped up the training session by advising, "Do your homework. Share what you have learned tonight with your family so they can help you with your dog's training. Practice every day. Call him to you while you're watching TV. Command him to sit or lie down periodically. When he comes, praise him, saying 'Good Come.' That reinforces what he did right. Then reward him every now and then with a treat to further reinforce his good behavior. This takes less of your time than having a half-hour practice session every night, and it teaches the dog that he is to obey all day, not just during practice sessions. Look at it as on-the-job training. Good luck."

As we were all leaving the class, Jenna caught my eye. "You look deep in thought. Do you have a question?"

"I'm sorry. I was just thinking about what you said about consistency and how it applies to my work."

"Want to talk about it?" She paused for a moment, and when I hesitated, said, "I apologize. I don't mean to pry."

"It's okay."

"Sometimes it's good to bounce your ideas off someone removed from the situation."

"Well, we are working on an important project, and my manager and I don't see things the same way. I'm afraid we are giving our staff mixed messages."

"You're right, Marti. That certainly can lead to confusion." I nodded yes. "You might also find other answers to your work problems right in our obedience class."

"No offense, Jenna, but people aren't like dogs. They can't be tricked into performing at your beck and call with a dog biscuit."

Jenna looked a little taken aback. "The object of dog training is not to trick them into doing what you want. It's about building a relationship based on clear communication and trust. If people in the corporate world treated one another with the same degree of openness, trust, and positive reinforcement that successful human-dog relationships enjoy, they would be a lot more productive."

I wasn't convinced, and she must have seen this in my face.

"I need help with managing people, too, Marti," she explained, "My father retired recently. He used to supervise the staff at the kennel, but now I'm running the boot camp." Jenna suddenly became more animated. "Tell you what, Marti, let's see how we can help each other. Maybe my training techniques can help you get your project back on track and you can help me get my staff in sync."

I was skeptical of Jenna's idea, but I was also desperate and there was something inherently trustworthy about her. What did I have to lose? Besides, I told myself, sometimes opportunities stare us straight in the face when we least expect it. Maybe I should give her a chance. "Okay, let's give it a try."

"Sounds great. When is your deadline?" Marti inquired.

"Six weeks."

"That matches our dog training schedule. Let's touch base after class each week to share ideas."

I couldn't believe that I was nodding in agreement. Would I really stake my career on the principles of dog training? Was I that desperate? Well, why not? I had nothing to lose. This project was going to the dogs anyway.

THE REST OF THE WEEK I PRACTICED WITH DEWEY AT HOME. When he came as called, he got a treat and he started to respond positively. He loved all the attention from me and from Hank as I demonstrated what I'd learned at dog obedience class.

Tuesday morning, I drove to work with renewed energy. I realized that although my staff had most of the facts, they hadn't pieced them together. Or maybe they had but were in denial. It's one thing to lay the facts out in front of them and hope they get it, but it's another thing to state my expectations clearly. And, if someone wandered too far off course, I had to be prepared to tug the leash.

I realized now that I had told my team I needed results in six weeks, but I didn't give them a specific deadline for revising the project plan. I hadn't even given them specific, quantifiable goals. Yet, somehow, I expected them to produce the results I wanted without understanding what needed to be done.

This time, I called everyone into the conference room to become completely aware of the situation and leave no room for doubt. "Listen up folks," I began, "Nate met with KFI on Friday, and we've been given six weeks to deliver results. You know that our overall company performance is down, so we can't afford to lose this account." Already, I could see Kevin rolling his eyes, but I continued. "What I need from you is a detailed project plan recommending how to accomplish this by the end of next month. Please include specific tasks and timelines, and I need your ideas by 3:00 this afternoon. We've made a lot of progress already, and now we need to find a way to make this happen."

I concluded the meeting by saying I'd meet with them individually to discuss their specific roles. Then I asked Kevin to join me in my office first. He closed the door and slumped into the chair facing my desk, letting out a sigh.

"Kevin, I need you to work closely with Grace to develop a final projection."

Kevin sighed again and clicked his tongue. "That's almost impossible in that time frame. Besides, Grace isn't that organized. She spends half her time digging through paper piles on her desk looking for notes. It'll take her until 3:00 tomorrow just to find everything she needs for this."

Here we are playing tug-of-war once again. But this time, I was ready. "Kevin, we need it done now." I was firm, looking him straight in the eyes without the slightest flinch. "You and Grace can meet that deadline only if you work together. I'll need it by 3:00."

After ten long seconds of silence, he replied, "As long as you put it that way, do you have any suggestions how we can do it?"

Kevin and I discussed the deliverables, and he didn't resist or complain. He sat and listened, asking an occasional question. I maintained eye contact while giving him clear directions. I was steadfast, but polite. While he wasn't happy with the deadline, we still managed to agree on exactly what needed to be done, when, and how we would proceed.

As Kevin left my office, I was amazed at what I just learned. I thought about what I had done differently this time. I was clear and firm about my expectations, and he agreed and left my office to get started. No complaining. No whimpering. No eye-rolling.

Now I realized the power of giving clear direction and of being firm about my expectations. I also sensed that my staff was starting to understand the sense of urgency that surrounded this project. Once I had called the meeting, told them specifically what I wanted, why it was important, and exactly when I needed it, the team began to collaborate. When Dewey and I had gotten into a tug-of-war the previous day, Jenna had said, "Be very clear about what you want and don't take no for an answer." With that, she checked Dewey's leash, and he obeyed willingly. The same thing had just happened with Kevin. Clarity, firmness, and a quick check on his attitude had effectively reined him in on his duties. I was on to something. His attitude might still need work, but this was a good beginning.

As Jenna trained the dogs, she had emphasized the importance of body language and a calm, firm voice. From the instant Kevin rolled his eyes, he had pushed my frustration level into the red zone. I had to stay calm with a firm tone of voice to snap him to attention and get the results I wanted. This experience with Kevin made me realize that, although I shouldn't correct his behavior constantly or aggressively, when the situation warrants it, I had to be firm. However, this tone of voice must be reserved for special situations. If overused, it loses its impact.

Paws for Reflection

Unclear expectations lead to confusion, frustration, insecurity, and mistakes.

Build a relationship based on clear communication and trust.

Notes

Paws for Reflection

Communicate your expectations clearly. Guide them in the right direction.

Chapter 3

Building a Sound Relationship: They've Got to Know You're Trustworthy

I ventured over to Nate's office to show him the new plan. Kevin and Grace had submitted theirs on time and, after reviewing it last night, I knew that it was in good shape.

"Hmm-mm," came his familiar voice from the open door. "Yeah, uh-huh. You bet! Take care now." Then I heard the phone receiver click.

"How's it going?" he queried as he saw me at his door

"Well, here is the revised project time estimate. But getting accurate time and cost estimates has been a real challenge."

"I just want a report that tells KFI that the project will be done by July 30. They're not pleased, and you don't seem to understand how close they are to giving us the boot," he retorted.

This remark put me on the defensive. "Our team worked hard on a revised plan, but based on the implementation plans for similar recent projects, six weeks is not enough. In fact, it's a major stretch. The team needs to understand why this time is different. I think I should tell them how bad things really are."

Nate's jaw dropped as if that were the most preposterous idea he'd ever heard. "Marti, why would you do a thing like that?"

"Because they have a right to know the whole situation."

"You'll only get people all panicky. They'll be gossiping and updating their LinkedIn profiles. I don't want our best and brightest bolting for the door or wasting energy worrying about anything other than the KFI project. Your people only need to know enough to keep them hustling on that implementation." Nate sat back and put his hands behind his head.

"Look, Marti, now is not the time to be open and honest with your people. And don't get all buddy-buddy with them either. Keep your distance. If you get to know them too well, they'll take advantage of you. The closer you get to them, the harder it will be if the worst comes to pass."

Nate lived in euphemisms—the words layoff, fire, termination, and dismissal weren't in his vocabulary. His comments were always couched in buzzwords, such as rightsizing, reorganization, improving efficiency, making difficult decisions.

The phone rang. Checking the caller ID, Nate said, "I have to take this." Waving me out with his left hand, he picked up the phone with his right. "I'll look over the plan, but as long as it has a completion date of July 30, that's all I care about."

On my way to work the next day—earlier than usual—I thought, it wasn't intentional, but I've kept my distance from our team. I've just been too busy to fraternize. *I didn't mean to be, but I've unintentionally been following Nate's advice all along. That was about to change.*

So much for my planned early arrival. It was already almost 8:30, and my inbox was bursting at the seams. My phone convulsed and beeped like an alarm. Before I could respond to even one, Grace popped her head in my door. "Marti, may I talk to you for a second?"

"Sure, come on in," I said in a flat tone.

Grace slid into the chair facing my desk. Her short auburn hair was in a pageboy cut that perfectly framed her heart-shaped face. She was somewhere in her thirties, but her rimless glasses made it hard to tell exactly where. She had an overflowing leather portfolio on her lap, many of the papers flagged with tiny Post It notes. "I just wanted to remind you that I have to leave early for lunch today. I have a parent-teacher conference, but I'll stay later tonight to keep the project moving."

"That's fine, thanks for letting me know," I responded in a monotone.

"See you later," she said and left.

A thought jolted me as Grace left: How rude I was. I barely looked at her while we were talking. My voice must have sounded as if I were bored to death. When I looked up from my computer, I noticed the photo of Dewey, and I thought of how he was learning to trust me as I spent more time with him and showed him that I cared for him. It dawned on me that I had been working with Grace for weeks and just now learned that she was a parent. Was she married? I didn't recall seeing a ring. And I didn't remember seeing any pictures of children on her desk. But then again, I usually summoned her from her cube and was in such a rush that I didn't notice such details when I visited her work area. In the short time I'd been here, I'd hit the ground running with my new team and was all business—all smart and no heart. I hadn't hired this team—I'd inherited them. I quickly assessed their respective skill levels, but what did I know about any of them personally? I expected them to give more than a third of their lives to our company; I should at least act a little interested in them as people. How can I expect to gain their trust when I appear to care so little about their lives?

The phone rang. It was Warren Sparks, my first boss at Prism and long-time mentor. I picked up. "Well, hello, Warren."

"Marti, how's it going?"

"Busy but hanging in there."

"I'm just confirming our lunch date."

I thought of declining but realized that perhaps Warren could help.

AT THE RESTAURANT, WARREN ASKED ME more about Hank, our beach house, and me. He was interested to learn about Dewey's training class. It was almost ten minutes before we got to the topic of work. Only then did I begin to bring him up to date on KFI and my dealings with Nate.

"There's no doubt that Nate is a different breed than I am," said Warren. "He knows everyone, but doesn't know anyone well. Prism hired him a couple of years ago for his massive contacts. You can't argue with his results. His consulting group has been Prism's cash cow since he came on board—at least until recently."

I had never heard Warren say anything bad about anyone, but his assessment of Nate was pushing his diplomacy to the limit.

"Marti, when it comes to dealing with my staff, you know I've always been a straight shooter. I tell it like it is. It's important to build relationships. There isn't a member of my team who hasn't been to my home or had lunch with me, one-on-one."

I smiled. "You are probably one of the best-liked and respected people at Prism, and you've certainly been a great mentor to me."

"I don't manage the way I do to be popular," he continued, "I do it out of respect. I'd rather be part of an effective team than a tyrant. My informal style builds trust throughout our group. I always try to find some common ground with each member of my team. Do you remember the common ground I found with you?"

"It was our love of dogs."

"That's right. The first time we went out to lunch, I noticed an SPCA brochure on your passenger seat."

"If I remember correctly, that turned out to be a three-hour lunch."

"The commitment and loyalty you've demonstrated over the years was well worth the extra-long lunch that day. Listen," he continued, "a manager can't be everyone's best friend, but your people deserve your respect, and that respect builds trust. I believe that trust grows over time. Imagine it as a pail of water. Every time you keep a promise or maintain a confidence, every time you are true to your word, you add a drop to the pail. When you demonstrate caring or concern by visiting with an individual or just being kind, you add another drop to the pail of trust. But if that trust is betrayed through untruths or lack of keeping promises, for example, it's like a massive leak in that pail, and trust is damaged."

I needed more of this kind of Warren's advice, but right now I was under pressure to perform, and in a hurry. "But what should I do about KFI? My team must suspect that things are not as rosy as Nate would lead them to believe. Other groups at Prism are quietly laying people off, and we lost several accounts that no one's talking about. The rumor mill is going full tilt. What would you do?"

"Well, keep in mind that I work with smaller clients and shorter duration projects. Our project plans and budget sheets are less complex, but all our spreadsheets, budgets, and project plans are in a common network drive. With the exception of salary, bonus, and performance-review information, my department has access to everything. I have nothing to hide. I don't treat my team like children, and I expect them not to act as such."

"What if they ask you about some kind of sensitive issue, point blank?" I asked.

"As long as it's not overly sensitive, or unless I am specifically instructed to keep something under wraps, I tell them. I try to be as open and honest as possible. If I know the answer, but am not permitted to give it, I promise to get back to them if it's appropriate. Or, as long as it's not something that's confidential, if they guess correctly, I won't deny it."

I nodded. He was making a lot of sense, and I trusted his instincts.

"Marti, managers often put off telling employees bad news because they're afraid that the top performers will be the first to run for the door. If you pump sunshine when everything is obviously falling apart, you'll lose credibility. And, once you've lost credibility, trust follows it out the door. But, if you have a strong basis of trust, people are more likely to stick by you in the difficult times."

"You know," I said. "it's not that different from training Dewey. Spending time with him and bonding with him has built a foundation of trust. It's time to start bonding with my team and letting them know how things stand."

Walking to the parking lot, Warren said, "You know, Marti, when I'm faced with a complex situation like yours, my dog gets a bonus walk. It gives me the time to slow down, breathe deep, and connect with the present moment. In that quiet time, it frees my mind. It's then and there where I find that true healing, inspiration, and problem-solving begin to flourish."

"That sounds a lot like mindfulness. I've been hearing so much about it lately," I said.

"That's exactly what it is. Dogs are paragons of mindfulness. They live in the moment, not concerned about the future or encumbered by the past. Their time on Earth is shorter than ours, and they make the most of it. They are accepting and forgiving, never holding grudges. They have a natural curiosity and see the world out there as something to discover and are open to new possibilities."

"Thanks," I said. "I'm looking forward to Dewey's next walk."

AFTER LUNCH, I CHECKED IN WITH GRACE to offer support. I reached for the phone to call her into my office and then decided to walk over to her cube instead. Through the mountains of desk clutter, I spotted a framed picture of her at the beach with a little boy, about six or seven years old I'd guess. Also there were several crayon drawings of seashells and dolphins pinned to the wall. "Grace, how's it going?"

"I'm still on target to have that report to you by 3:00."

"Great! How did things go at the school?" I suddenly realized that until a few minutes ago, I didn't even know if she had a boy or a girl or more than one child. Then I wondered if maybe the question was too personal.

Grace looked a little stunned, then smiled. "Nicholas is doing fine. His teacher recommended him for the gifted program next year."

"That's wonderful! What grade is he in?"

"He's in second grade."

"What does he want to be when he grows up?"

"He wants to be a marine biologist." Caught off guard, Grace paused for a moment. "He's already obsessed with sharks. He checks out all the shark books he can find at the library, and I record all the Discovery Channel shows about sharks for him."

"It sounds like he just might be the next Jacques Cousteau."

We both stared at the photo for a few seconds. This interaction with Grace gave me a better sense of the full context of her life. Then I came back to business. "I just wanted to see if you needed any help. Is everything on track with the project plan?"

Grace nodded. "Yes. 3:00 it is."

"Great! Let me know if you have any questions."

"I will. Thanks."

At exactly 3:00, Grace stopped by my office. "Hello, Grace. Come on in."

"I emailed you the report a few minutes ago. Did you get it?"

"Yes, I was just reviewing it."

"Well, I do have some concerns. Do you have a minute?"

"Sure, please sit down."

"We really don't think we can deliver in six weeks. But frankly, Nate intimidates everyone on the team. We feel we need to tell him and KFI what they want to hear even if it's not quite the truth. Personally, I'm not comfortable with that. This work plan delivers the minimum viable project requirements completed in six weeks. But there are several major disadvantages."

I was pleased with Grace's honesty. "Go on."

"The first problem is that there is absolutely no room for error with this plan. The second is that, unless we can get two more resources immediately, all the team members will have to work non-stop, including every weekend, to meet the deliverables." She paused a minute, then asked, "Well, what do you think?"

"Well, I appreciate your honesty. I'll review the report and then go into further detail with Nate and get back to you. Thanks for all your hard work on this."

A moment after Grace left, my eyes wandered to the picture of Dewey on my desk. The Dewey at the time that photo was taken was not the same Dewey that I know today. That Dewey didn't yet trust me, but that's improved a little as I've spent more time with him over the last few days. Similarly, by beginning to build rapport with Grace, I had helped her to trust me a little more. I felt that if I hadn't had that personal conversation with Grace, we wouldn't have had this open and honest chat. Although I knew I couldn't build our team's trust overnight, little moments of bonding—like this one—would begin to lay the groundwork for a solid long-term foundation of trust.

Paws for Reflection

Honest communication builds the foundation for trust.

Earn their trust and loyalty will follow.

Notes

Paws for Reflection

Without trust you can't build a positive, long-lasting relationship.

Notes

Paws for Reflection

Hold yourself accountable first.
Lead by example.

Accountability increases personal credibility and improves morale and performance.

Notes

Chapter 4

Leadership: Be a Master First, a Friend Second

Most of Dewey's classmates were already in the barn by the time we arrived for our lesson. Most, but not all. A moment later, Buddy, the sheepdog, bolted into the room, dragging Sue behind him. Dozens of eyes turned to the struggling pair. Sue tugged Buddy's leash to get him under control, but the unruly, walking mop was still tugging, however less than the previous week.

"You've been practicing," said Jenna, entering the room. "You're making progress, Sue. Now check his leash one more time. Be firm—don't just tug." Sue jerked the leash firmly and, to her surprise, Buddy slowed down and waited for her to catch up. Willingly, he followed Sue perhaps for the first time in his life. She walked Buddy over next to Dewey and me.

"Looks like you're walking Buddy instead of the other way around," I said to her.

"Thanks," she replied, beaming.

I thought of Kevin the other day when I had to tug his invisible chain a bit to get his attention. *Amazing, it really does work. When I was clear about my expectation and held my ground, he responded positively instead of whining.*

Clearing her throat, Jenna said, "Today, I'd like to emphasize the most important aspect of training a dog—leadership. Guidance and direction occur naturally in a pack," she reminded us. "Every dog knows who's in charge—who's the alpha dog. Dogs are willing to accept the leader; what they don't understand is a lack of leadership. When no dog takes the alpha role in a dog pack, chaos ensues until leadership is re-established." Jenna continued. "This is also true for your relationship with your pet. If you are not obviously in control, the dog will assume you have abdicated your role as top dog. Dogs instinctively look for someone to be in charge. If there's a leadership void—no obvious top dog—another dog will try to take charge."

Rob, the owner of a large rottweiler named Winston, asked, "Do all dogs want to be top dog?"

"No," Jenna replied. "Some dogs are more dominant by nature and will always try to take charge. Most others are glad to follow the leader, but they need guidance. Without it, they will try to assume command and take charge. In the same way, if you were a passenger in a car and the driver fell asleep, you would most likely grab the wheel."

I thought about my work situation. I was the new designated top dog. My team had been without a manager for about a month before I came on board. Nate had been their temporary supervisor, but he kept his distance. Since I was new in this department, my team was still getting used to me. True, Nate was still their Division Manager, but he was their leader in title only. Without a doubt, there had been a leadership void. And Kevin was vying to be the alpha dog.

I turned my attention back to class.

Jenna proceeded, "The symptoms of a dog taking charge may not be obvious at first. The dog may be less responsive when you call him, may saunter back to you, and then stop along the way to water the bushes. He might disregard a command like DOWN and pretend he didn't hear it."

"That's what Winston does!" Rob commented. "When I call him, he takes his time walking back to me, sniffing every object along the way. What can I do about it?"

"You need to take charge," Jenna explained. "The more you tolerate that kind of behavior, the more difficult Winston will be to control. He could eventually become aggressive and possibly growl or even bite. Every time you interact with your dog, either you're training it or it's teaching you."

"But how do we take charge?" asked Sue.

"You must establish yourself as the leader. It's very possible for a dog to love you and be loyal to you, but still not respect you as the leader of the pack. For example, you can't expect your dog to see you as his leader if you comply with his every request without requiring him to do something in return. If your dog nudges you and you pet him every time he does this, he thinks he commanded you to pet him and you obeyed."

The class chuckled.

"I've run into something similar with Dewey," I chimed in. "I'm always tripping over him in the hallway where he likes to nap. But I've always heard, *Let sleeping dogs lie.*"

"Marti, if you step around your dog when he's sleeping in the hall, he sees this as a sign of submission and assumes he's in charge. Good luck getting him to obey if you are constantly accommodating him by walking over and around him. "Next time he's in the way, command him to 'MOVE!' Nudge him with your foot first. If that doesn't work, attach the leash to lead him to another location if necessary. After a few times, he will then know that you're in charge and he'll clear out of your way. You must make your leadership position clear."

"But it seems so easy when you do it," Sue protested, her forehead wrinkled in frustration. She obviously didn't feel confident in pulling this one off at home.

"Then make him earn everything from his food to his pat on the head until he understands that you're in charge. Command him to SIT, LIE DOWN, STAY, or do some trick before you do whatever he wants—whether it's to eat or go out or play fetch."

Jenna continued, "I've said it before, and I'll say it again. Be clear about your expectations. Use simple commands like SIT, DOWN and STAY, with appropriate hand gestures like this." Sweeping her arm from the shoulder all the way down, she said, "DOWN!" Almost half the dogs in the room laid down. The class laughed.

"Remember, dogs need a little time to process information, so don't talk in complete sentences, and don't keep repeating the command. Say it once like you mean it—like a top dog—and expect him to comply. Then give him ten seconds to respond. If he doesn't do what you have requested, re-emphasize what you want him to do, as Sue just did with Buddy. Check his leash and indicate what you want, or step on the leash to get him to lie down," Jenna instructed as she approached Winston.

She held his leash loosely in her right hand and commanded, "Winston, DOWN!" simultaneously slowly moving her hand downward. When the stubborn rottweiler didn't comply, she repeated the command and gently stepped on his leash with her left foot, applying downward pressure. Jerking his head upward, Winston resisted, but when he eventually had no choice except to lie down or choke, he did as commanded. The instant he lay down, Jenna responded by patting his head, saying, "Winston, good down."

Jenna then explained to the class, "Notice that I began with his name, then the command, then, finally, the hand gesture. When he did as directed, his behavior was reinforced with 'Winston, good down.' Now, you try it."

I looked Dewey straight in the eye as I commanded, "Dewey, DOWN," then motioned with my hand. Panting, he stared at me blankly as if to say, "You've got to be kidding." Others in the class weren't doing much better.

Jenna came over to me, holding out her hands for Dewey's leash. "May I?" she asked.

"Dewey, DOWN," she said, gradually stepping on his leash. The instant he lay down, she said, "Good down, Dewey," and patted him on the head.

I realized this instant feedback was an essential part of training. The dogs responded to it favorably and behaved better when they received praise for doing things right. Being specific about what they did right also reinforced positive behavior.

"Now, try again with your foot on the leash," Jenna suggested.

"Dewey, DOWN!" I commanded again as I motioned with my hand and stepped gently on his leash. It didn't take long before he knew what DOWN meant.

"That's impressive," said Sue, "but what about when you're sitting, say at the dinner table, and you want your dog to lie down and stop begging?"

I was all ears. If begging were an Olympic event, Dewey would win the gold medal.

"Get him to obey the DOWN command with your foot on the leash, as we just demonstrated," Jenna answered. "Then keep your foot on the leash so he can't get up. He'll correct himself as the leash becomes taut every time he tries to get up. Ignore him as he feels the pressure from the leash and tries to resist. Then, when he settles down, praise him. Eventually, he'll learn what is expected."

We all tried the DOWN command some more, and even sat on a bench along the wall and practiced the leash stepping technique while our dogs were lying by our sides. To our surprise, it worked. After trying to resist a few times, our dogs were actually lying calmly.

"That's it for tonight," Jenna said. "You're all making good progress."

As the class members and their four-footed companions left, Jenna said, "Marti, how are things going with your project?"

"Funny you should ask. I was just thinking about the importance of giving clear direction as a leader. You were very firm and direct about what you expected Dewey to do just now—and it worked. I used the same technique with Kevin this past week, and it was successful." I explained to Jenna the situation with Kevin. "I have to establish myself as top dog if I expect to lead the pack!" I said. "Just like dogs can love their owners but not respect them, employees can like a manager as a person, even as a friend, but not respect them as their leader."

"You're right," Jenna agreed. "A manager or director's position has a certain level of authority, but some employees may resist or even challenge you, just as Winston had initially resisted the DOWN command."

"Leadership involves influencing others, and to do that you must earn credibility and respect. My team doesn't respect Nate. They're afraid of him."

Jenna furrowed her brow. "Why?"

"Well, Nate's idea of a 'team player' is someone who never disagrees with him. So they're more focused on doing what they think will appease him rather than what's best for the project."

"Believe it or not, I'm in a similar situation," Jenna said. My dad's been retired for less than a year and, while most of the staff respects my dog training skills, they still think of me as the boss's daughter. What I'm wrestling with, Marti, is how do I get them to respect me as their leader?"

"Gaining respect can be challenging. Different people respect different things. But providing clear direction is a good start just as you said it is with dog training."

"That makes sense." Jenna pursed her lips as she thought to herself. "Focus is important. The staff here at the Kennel need something more—purpose. In addition to knowing what they are expected to do, they need to know why. That's where leadership becomes most important for me."

Marti grinned. "I didn't say it was easy. I'm trying to give my team a vision for this project. I've started to do this, but Nate insists that each team member submits ridiculously detailed status reports weekly. This mandatory busywork sends the wrong information about priorities, and they lose sight of the project. That reminds me of something that happened last week. I grabbed my purse to look for something, and Dewey bolted for the door. He associated my picking up the purse with going for a ride, and he was ready to go. Ironically, I was only doing some online shopping."

"Employees do the same thing. They watch leaders for cues," Jenna added.

Dewey curled up at my feet, apparently worn out by all the excitement of the class. "You bet. Every time a manager walks through a room or a hallway, staff members look for clues like facial expressions to see if they're having a good or bad day. They watch whom managers talk to on the way to a meeting and how they respond when they talk to you."

"Like my canine students, they understand body language. "

"Exactly. If a manager is always late for meetings and takes two-hour lunches, he's sending employees the wrong message."

"Actions speak louder than words. Well, it's getting late. See you next week," Jenna replied as she waved good-bye.

As I walked back to the car with Dewey in tow, I wondered what kind of unintentional signals I was sending to my team. I was now more aware that my team members were constantly testing to see if I was really listening, if I cared about them as people, or if I just saw them as robots to do the mundane work. We really do lead by our actions.

On the way home, my mind was racing. When employees sense a lack of leadership, some may try to take over—maybe blatantly and other times in more indirect ways. Like passive-aggressive Kevin with his tug-of-war games and constant complaining.

If we ignore negative employee behavior such as bullying, missing deadlines, or being unproductive, it's like "stepping over the dog." It communicates a lack of leadership—a sign of weakness or submission. Employees are in control. The dogs are walking the owner.

ALTHOUGH IT WAS ONLY A LITTLE PAST 7:00 A.M., Nate's Benz was already in the office parking lot and I was greeted by another "See me" text from him the minute I entered the building. Bracing myself for bad news, I knocked on Nate's half-open door. Miraculously, he was not on the phone. "Marti, I have great news! KFI signed another contract for the Advanced Accounting module. That's gonna help the bottom line."

"So you bought us more time?" I asked.

"No." He looked at me, confused, tilting his head and squinting his eyes.

"We'll have to revise the work plan that we just finished. Advanced Accounting will take time to implement. We have to go back and change every screen shot in our training guides, slide presentations, and documentation. Everything has to be rewritten. It could take weeks," I protested.

"As far as KFI is concerned, the original deadline remains the same. It was the only way we could get them to buy the add-on. Find things to drop from the project that aren't mission critical."

"But we've already streamlined it to the bare bones. I'm concerned about the quality of work if we cut it too much."

"I'm sure you'll find a way." His phone conveniently rang. Saved by the bell. I got up and left.

On the drive home, I saw the day become a blur, just like the trees on the side of the road as I sped past them. It felt like I was chasing my tail. I feared that this project would be a disaster that would blow up in my face. My anxiety escalated as I imagined the company going out of business. I pictured everyone out of work. And it would all be my fault because we couldn't get the project done by the deadline. Granted it was a deadline based on fantasy, but no one wanted to know that, especially Nate, and certainly not the client.

Hank wasn't home when I arrived. Dewey barked happily, and I could hear his toenails scrape against the door as I slid the key into the lock. Petting Dewey, I reached for my phone out of habit to check email. I stopped. *Not this time.* I put the phone down on the counter. Grabbing the leash, I clasped it to Dewey's collar and out the door we went. Recalling Warren's mindfulness comments, I took a deep breath, cleared my mind, and we set off on a walk. We explored a different neighborhood than our usual route. We kept going, long after Dewey did his business.

With each stride, I was able to step out of the turbulent stream that was KFI and see it from the bank. Shifting myself from participant to observer, I discerned what was really happening and, for the first time, things didn't appear hopeless. Then it happened. I couldn't fathom why, but I was suddenly filled with determination, even elation. Had I just sunk so far to the bottom that there was nowhere else to go but up? Perhaps. But suddenly I saw a new perspective and new possibilities. Somehow I knew we would find a way for this to work. We would not only make that deadline—we would delight KFI with our innovative, top quality work.

Paws for Reflection

Earn their respect. Lead by your actions.

Establish yourself as top dog: Be the leader of the pack.

Notes

Chapter 5

Feedback, Rewards and Motivation

I hate getting to meetings late. It really irks me when other people do it. But just before my team meeting, Nate called me into his office for a "quick" update—five minutes of my updating—constantly interrupted by fifteen minutes of him taking phone calls while I sat there wasting precious time and worrying about how I was to convey the added workload to my team. Nate had agreed to it without giving a thought to how this could demoralize my team members. They were now on a steady roll, and their morale was improving. The best I could do was to tell them the truth without communicating my own aggravation. I would have to try to absorb the brunt internally and not lay too much on them. That's the burden of middle management—absorbing the frustrations of the team while shouldering the pressure from above.

I rushed to the meeting room, crafting my information. Laughter spilled into the hallway. Obviously, they were not working on our project, but it was nice to hear other people having fun in the office. I looked forward to the time that we could have more fun and actually enjoy our work again, but it didn't look like that was going to happen soon.

I ran into the full conference room at ten minutes past eleven. I didn't look at Kevin, but I sensed his eyes rolling as I took my seat. "Sorry about that," I said. No one said a word. I started the meeting. "Next week, we're going onsite at KFI. We will be there five days a week until Omega goes live."

"We're not prepared," Kevin interrupted.

"Then we have to get as prepared as we can. Certain events need to happen within this time frame. And I must tell you that we have an additional challenge. In his efforts to appease the client, Nate has committed us to adding on the Advanced Accounting module.

"How much more time do we have to do it?" The group seemed to ask the same question simultaneously.

"The time frame stays the same." They groaned in unison as I continued. "I realize that this is a tight schedule, tighter than we've ever faced. Each one of you has proven yourself on other projects. Now is the time to pull together and identify what needs to be done. Let's start with a review of commitments. Kevin, you go first."

"I've come up with a timetable for the data conversion. It will take five days to enter the data into the new system."

I furled my brow in confusion. "Your original plan called for nine or ten days."

"I made a few calls and found an ally at KFI who wants to meet this deadline as much as we do. He has committed some of his team to help with the project."

"That's great, Kevin. Thanks for being proactive on that."

Kevin smiled and nodded, and not in his usual snarky way. His attitude was encouraging.

"Alex, why don't you report?"

"I've completed most of the conversion and migration documentation. Now I'm working on the training materials. And I still need to meet with the system implementers that are already onsite to review and approve the docs."

"Have you set up a meeting with them?"

"Um, no."

"You need to get to that today."

"Will do."

I continued with a review of the project goals. I listed the goals on a flipchart in order of priority and explained the rationale for each.

I could see them nodding their heads as the energy level began to build. The project objectives were beginning to make sense to them. They understood how the objectives fit into the larger organization and its goals. The team began firing questions and ideas so quickly I couldn't record them on the flipchart fast enough.

Then I gave them a printout of the various metrics to use to measure our progress—or lack of it. These were not the measures that Nate used in his lengthy reports, but measures that relate to their daily work. That's when they started to really catch on. I began to hear comments such as:

"Oh, I didn't realize that was so important."

"We sure need to improve on this one."

"Wow, I didn't know we completed that many proposals this quarter."

I then asked how we could revise the reports further to keep each team member effectively informed of the team's total progress, not just their individual activities.

"Let's incorporate our individual status reports into the project work plan and place them in the common drive so we can all see what others are doing," suggested Grace.

"Great idea!" said Kevin. "But what about Nate? He won't like the idea that we've changed the reporting system."

I was so surprised at Kevin's support of Grace that I paused before I said, "Let me handle Nate."

We recorded tasks and due dates and assigned deliverables. I closed the meeting by thanking everyone for their special efforts. But before we adjourned, I said, "Kevin and Grace, thank you for your prompt work on revising the KFI work plan. I know that it was extremely tight, but I really appreciate your effort in making this happen."

I even spent some time talking to Kevin about his family after the meeting. His son, Tim, was heading to college in fall and his wife, Louise, was beginning to suffer from the empty nest syndrome. It felt good to start building a more positive relationship with Kevin and, for the first time, I was actually beginning to believe that this project was going to work out.

In my previous job, I had taken my high-functioning team for granted—nothing had to be spelled out. We had strong synergy. But that came from years of working together and understanding not only one another's strengths and weaknesses, but also work styles. Developing those kinds of relationships takes time—time we didn't have right now. But establishing a two-way communication system was certainly a start. The revised reports would provide an instant feedback system, a feedback system just like the pooches in training trying to get up while their leashes were firmly planted under the owners' feet.

But feedback is not just about reinforcing positive behavior. When performance isn't satisfactory, constructive feedback is in order.

LATER THAT DAY, I HAD SCHEDULED TIME with Alex to discuss his performance. He had missed a few deadlines in getting information to Kevin and Grace for the revised work plan. That, in turn, created obstacles to meeting KFI's timeline, and this was not a good time to be falling behind. He also should have scheduled a meeting with the system implementers without being told, so he was in the doghouse.

As I prepared for my discussion with Alex, I started to get cold feet. I needed to energize myself to follow through on this. *I'm not the first manager to deal with this,* I encouraged myself. It's not easy to tell an employee something negative about his performance to his face. But not doing so is unfair to both the employee and the manager. Suddenly, it dawned on me that it's cheating me most of all. *That's why I'd been getting so many stomach aches.* If I'm not honest with my own employees, I feel the anguish inside. It seems like avoiding the issues is the easy way out, but instead, it gnaws at me from the inside out.

As hard as it may be, a manager needs to be upfront and discuss problems directly with individuals. It's certainly not an easy job.

Alex arrived at my office door for our meeting, and I invited him to take a seat. He slouched into the chair.

"Alex, how is it going with the system implementers? Did you get the documents to them for review?"

He hesitated. "Most of them," he hedged.

"The project plan calls for all of the docs to be in review by now."

"I sent some of it to them. They're not answering my phone calls or e-mails. They're totally blowing me off."

"How much of it did you send?"

"Sections one and two, and the first part of three."

"They're supposed to be done reviewing all five sections by now."

Alex protested. "I've been working really hard, and I'm doing the best I can."

"I know you're trying hard, but I believe you can do better. The work plan says that all five sections are done and in review. This is not the case?"

Hesitantly, Alex nodded.

"And you didn't get your input on the work plan to Kevin and Grace on time. Alex, from what I know about you so far, you're an extremely talented technical writer and trainer."

"Uh, thanks."

"Your time management and project management skills need some work, though. If you're not meeting your deliverables, I expect you to let me know. Don't just tell me what you think I want to hear. Your status reports need to accurately reflect what's going on from your end."

Alex squirmed in his seat. "I thought I could catch up to the deliverable dates before anyone noticed. I just didn't want to get into trouble."

I took a deep breath. "There'll be more trouble if the team isn't as far along as I believe it is. And inaccurate reporting undermines trust on the team. We have to be honest with each other."

"I'm so used to telling Nate what he wants to hear, I guess I just continued the pattern with you."

"I expect your reports to be accurate in the future. What are some action steps we can take to make sure that happens?"

"I can see that I need to be more realistic about my project time estimates."

"That's a start. Your work plan calls for forty hours a week for two straight weeks of writing. Do you anticipate being in any meetings during those two weeks?"

"I probably spend eight hours in meetings each week."

"How about taking phone calls and answering e-mails? All of these activities are necessary, yet they eat into your writing time." I took a sip of water.

"But you said this was a tight time frame."

"I did. But, Alex, having status reports that say the project is on time, when it isn't true, doesn't help us meet deadlines. The reports need to be accurate, not just best case scenarios. When you approach a project, look at each task. Can you miss some of the regular meetings or attend for just the part that is most relevant to your work? How much time can you realistically devote to a particular task in a single day? What is the worst case scenario that could delay or extend that task?"

Alex hung his head slightly. "I understand. If I fall behind again, I'll let you know."

"I know you've been successful in earlier projects. The bottom line is this: Our customers need to be satisfied, and we need to meet our deliverables when we say we will. You play a critical role in achieving this goal."

Alex and I talked a while longer. He offered some excuses, but also a few good ideas. I suggested that we enroll him in formal project management training when we complete the KFI project. We mutually agreed that he would keep track of due dates more closely, advise others in advance when he needed something, and prioritize tasks more carefully.

THE WEEK FLEW BY QUICKLY. Before I knew it, I was in dog training class again.

Jenna called the class to attention saying, "When our canine companions misbehave, they need instant feedback. If you don't communicate your displeasure, problem dogs will assume that everything is fine and continue that behavior until it is addressed. And when you give feedback, you reinforce the desired behavior. For example, immediately following the command 'NO,' when a dog stops whatever negative behavior he was doing, praise the dog for obeying. A simple pat on the head will reinforce the desired behavior which will likely be repeated. Whether the feedback is positive or negative," Jenna warned, "it must be timely. With dogs, feedback has no impact at all seconds after they've done something wrong because they don't remember what they did fifteen seconds ago. They are incapable of understanding that what they did was good or bad unless you catch them in the act. It's got to be real-time feedback."

Throughout the class, Jenna was quick to praise. When Dewey did what he was supposed to do, she patted him on the head and enthusiastically said, "Good boy, Dewey, good boy!" She was equally quick to admonish him when necessary.

After class, Jenna approached me. "How's the project going?" she asked.

"Getting there, but it could be better. Giving feedback is so much easier with dogs than humans. There's no big discussion, no excuses, no emotions, and no politics to deal with. You basically communicate your needs, and they follow the direction of the Top Dog if we've successfully established our superiority in the pack."

"The concept common to both man and beast is the need for feedback," added Jenna. "What we reinforce or encourage is exactly what we will get in the future."

"Constructive feedback can certainly improve an employee's work performance. I'm even seeing a little improvement in Kevin since I've been giving him honest feedback on his behavior."

"While a dog doesn't remember what he did fifteen seconds later, our employees certainly have much longer memories. But it's still essential to give feedback in a timely manner for the best results. Feedback can build people's skills and reinforce their confidence."

"It can also make them feel insecure if the feedback is unclear or destructive," I concluded.

"Dogs are definitely eager to please and seem genuinely happy when they do things right." Jenna emphasized, "Along with food, praise is his salary and toys are like bonuses. Bonuses for a job well done are appreciated in the canine world as much as in the business world."

I agreed. "But the rewards don't have to be monetary—or treats in the case of dogs. So why don't we remember to give our employees encouragement and praise more frequently?"

"That's a good question," Jenna admitted.

My discussion with Jenna gave me a lot to think about on the way home. We sometimes forget that everyone likes to be recognized for doing a good job. Feedback is a key component to communicate what is right or wrong. What is good or bad behavior for dogs? What is good or bad work performance?

While both dogs and employees need feedback and encouragement, it seems more obvious with dogs. Without feedback and attention, employees and dogs can sometimes act out in a negative way. Many managers believe that since employees are getting paid to do a job, that's enough. Managers also assume employees know when they're doing a good job and sometimes forget that employees need recognition and rewards, too. And don't wait until the annual performance review, which often doesn't happen on time or maybe not at all.

I made a mental note to remember to follow up and give Alex feedback on his progress the next day and to encourage him on what went well. After all, we all need positive feedback once in a while.

Later that week, I sent the team an e-mail redirecting the project status meeting to Le Bistro, a restaurant not far from the office.

Nate was dressed for the golf course a few days later when I entered his office for our status meeting. For once, he wasn't on the phone.

"What's this I hear about a two-hour lunch at LeBistro today?" he demanded.

"I want to recognize the team for all their hard work," I countered. "We not only caught up to the plan, but we're actually getting a little ahead of schedule. We're just about ready for next week's on-site."

"Look, save the recognition routine for later when Omega's up and running at KFI. We don't have the time or the money for extravagances like this. Other teams will talk and expect similar treatment."

"But my people deserve it. They're working nights and weekends to bring this project in on schedule under tough circumstances. In fact, I'd like to see if we could arrange a project completion bonus like we did for my last project team. My former boss, Warren, always budgeted extra funds for those who consistently exceed expectations. He called it the Extra Mile fund."

"I'm not Warren." Nate shrugged, shaking his head from side to side. "I expect my people to excel on a regular basis. There shouldn't be special treatment for merely meeting expectations."

"But it's that kind of recognition that keeps them motivated to perform at a high level." I wanted to allude to the rumored five-figure bonus Nate received last year, but now was not the time.

"Their reward is that they still have a job."

"Nate, what's the percentage of our implementations completed on or close to schedule?"

"Less than twenty percent. But that's usually because the client changes the project scope."

"KFI has changed scope more than a few times since this project began."

"True."

"So would you say this trend is likely to continue?"

"It shouldn't."

"But it could?"

Nate nodded.

"So if you think it's not likely that the team will meet all of the objectives to KFI's satisfaction by the scheduled launch date, what's the harm in offering our team a little incentive? If they meet the deadline under these conditions, they deserve a bonus."

"All right, you can announce a project-completion bonus to your team. But results absolutely, positively must be delivered on time. It's all or nothing. No exceptions."

"Thank you! Thank you. You won't regret this."

"Yeah, yeah. Now get moving. You don't want to miss your fancy luncheon."

My team is always punctual when food is involved, so predictably they were seated in a back room at Le Bistro shortly before noon.

I stood and said, "Today I wanted to prove that not every meeting these days is about bad news. True, KFI is not ready to sing our praises, and we're a long way from being out of the woods with them. But, we're making progress, and I want to thank you all for your efforts so far. And, although bonuses have been in short supply this year, I've arranged to set some money aside to celebrate the completion of this project, but only if the implementation is completed on time and KFI is happy with us. Are you up for this?"

Everyone nodded. Kevin even said, "Yes," out loud.

I felt like a general rallying the troops.

Paws for Reflection

*Use sincere praise
as a motivator.*

*Reinforce your expectations.
Provide constructive,
timely feedback.*

Notes

Paws for Reflection

Constructive feedback improves performance and it doesn't cost a dime.

Connect a reward with a specific behavior.

Notes

Chapter 6

Discipline and Consequences

KFI had promised us a designated office suite, but their tiny "war room" was ill-equipped for us to wage much of a war. The desks weren't even the same color or height and one was even missing a leg. The chairs around the conference table didn't match. This was where office furniture came to die.

The war room was a long, narrow room with windows along one side and a door at each end. Tables lined each side of the room, so half of us faced the window and the other half faced the wall. Situated at the far east end of their campus, we were as far as we could be from the heart of the action and still be on the KFI grounds.

Our work space was the least of our problems. Corporate security didn't have badges ready for us when we arrived, and we wasted an hour just waiting to get into the building. Our laptops couldn't log us on to KFI's systems, and there weren't enough phones for all of us. These obstacles chipped away at what little lead we had gained.

It was time for a meeting with Tyler Harding, KFI's IT Project Manager. Our team walked down the hall, trying to find the conference room on his floor.

"Well, it's certainly a bit snazzier than our own digs," Grace muttered to no one in particular as we stopped outside Tyler's office.

Tyler greeted us in the hall. At over six feet, he was an imposing figure with a disarming smile. With glasses, reddish beard, and plaid shirt, he reminded me of an intellectual lumberjack. "Good morning, nice to see you, Marti." He led us into a modern, dark-paneled room with a long rectangular table in the center. After we introduced one another, he got down to business.

"As you know, I'll be managing the implementation from Kramer's side. I'll be your go-to person for anything you need from our end." Smiling, he offered, "Please don't hesitate to ask for anything that you can think of to keep the project on track."

We mentioned some of the issues with log-on capability and discussed other equipment we would be need.

"OK, we will get those issues resolved. Now let's review some of the commitments for this week. We're four weeks from our targeted "go-live" date—the date we will actually start running the new software. And that means that we want training delivered about a week before that. Which one of you is responsible for it?"

"That would be me," Alex replied.

"How is it coming along?"

"I have most of the documentation completed. I just need to touch base with some of the users for testing. Also, which facilities should we use for the classes?"

"What? You haven't reserved the training rooms yet?" interrupted Kevin.

"I was going to—" Alex stuttered in amazement at Kevin's outburst.

"You were going to what?" Kevin shouted. "These people need advance notice so they can get the training classes on their calendars. The training rooms need to be reserved. Get with the program."

A stunned silence filled the room. Grace cringed as Alex looked to the floor. I wanted to throttle Kevin. But it would have to wait until we were alone.

Tyler got up from his chair and, backing out of the room, said, "Uh, if any of you need me, you have my number."

"Kevin, let's have a word in the hall." I bit my lip as I tried hard to control my anger.

He followed me down the hall and around the corner where we couldn't be overheard.

"Kevin, I can't believe you did that." I practically hissed at Kevin.

"Did what?"

"You belittled Alex, not just in front of our team, but in front of the client."

"Alex is dragging us down. All of his deliverables are behind schedule. I don't want us to miss our deadline because he dropped the ball."

"It's my job to provide that feedback to him, not yours. And certainly not in front of Tyler!"

"I thought we're supposed to be a team. I was just giving feedback from one player to another."

"It was not the time or the place."

He just looked at me and—you guessed it—rolled his eyes.

Before he could also sigh, my phone rang showing Nate's number.

I looked back to where Kevin had been, but he had already stormed down the hall. I could feel the heat on the back of my neck. I was annoyed, but this matter would have to wait. I had to deal with Nate first.

I was pleasantly shocked when, later on, Kevin stopped by my office.

"Look, I'm sorry about what happened. I should have talked to Alex about it in private. I guess I wanted Tyler to see that we could get the job done."

"You don't accomplish that by bullying one of your own team members, especially in front of a client."

"I know," he said clearly subdued. Kevin looked weary; his head hung low, the cockiness gone.

"I appreciate your apology, but I think you owe one to Alex as well. He's making headway. Maybe instead of intimidating him into finishing his tasks, you should see what you can do to help him complete them. It will only benefit the whole team in the long run."

Kevin nodded. "I know I'm a pain to deal with."

I didn't disagree. I didn't say anything.

He continued, "I'm a pretty good software developer, but I realize that sometimes I say things that put people off. I know we can't afford to lose KFI, and I don't want this project to fall apart because I said something stupid. What can I do to help make this right?"

"Well, you can start by helping me smooth things over with Tyler and by being more civil with your own team members. I realize you want what's best for the project, and you're often right when you speak your mind, but you need to develop some tact."

"I've heard that before," he muttered to the floor.

"Think before you speak. Ask yourself, *Will this make Prism look bad? Could my remark offend someone?*"

"I'll really work at it. I don't feel good about what happened."

This was the second time I had to deal with Kevin's bullying. It had to stop. He meant well for the project, but he was destroying morale.

Jenna told us that a leash correction combined with an emphatic NO! is most effective. One firm leash check is better than ten slight tugs.

If your dog jumps on a house guest, a firm leash correction will get it to stop the unwanted behavior, while a half-hearted OFF will often have little impact, especially if your voice is not stern. The dog will discern that you don't really mean it and will disregard your command. However, if you tug his leash and say OFF! with a strict tone and firm look, he'll know you mean business and will obey. Likewise, for obstinate or aggressive employees like Kevin, a firm, authoritative tone of voice and a strong admonition are just the right ticket to get your point across when someone gets out of line.

Jenna also emphasized that for more cooperative dogs, a softer tone of voice and gentle check will suffice. When an employee commits a slight indiscretion, something like, "C'mon, Alex, you know you shouldn't do that," will probably work.

THE LAST THING I HAD TIME FOR WAS LUNCH with Warren. I was just about to call to cancel when he phoned me.

"We still on?" he asked. I could picture his grin.

"I really shouldn't. I have so much to do."

Warren has a way of influencing people to do what he wants while making them feel like it was their idea. I was still objecting as I talked on my phone, walking to my car to meet him for lunch.

As usual, he beat me to the restaurant. He was already sitting at a table near the front when I walked in, smiling as we made eye contact.

"How do you get everything done and have time for lunch?" I asked. "You have at least as much work on your plate as I do, yet you sit here calmly like you haven't a care in the world."

"It's a gift. How's it going?"

I told him about setting up at Kramer and Franton, the logistical problems, and Kevin's latest unfortunate outburst.

"Look, you're making headway. This'll be over before you know it. How goes the dog training?"

I laughed. "Dewey's taking to it pretty well. Ironically, last night we talked about consistency and discipline."

"How appropriate." He grinned.

"Jenna emphasized that dogs learn much faster when they know what to expect. Consistency in enforcing the rules is extremely important."

"It's the same way with your team," Warren said. "Look at Kevin. He hasn't had the same boss for more than a couple of years throughout his twenty-year stint at Prism. Nobody's properly coached or counseled him, and he's been able to get away with being an office bully all this time."

"I'm hoping to change that. We had a breakthrough this morning."

"Marti, it's all about consistency. Without it, long-time behavior won't change. And if a manager is inconsistent, the resulting confusion leads to discipline problems and feelings of favoritism and unfairness. You know what it can do to morale."

I took a sip of water. "It's the same problem when each family member trains a dog differently or when two managers send mixed signals to their direct reports."

"You're sure getting a lot of mileage from your dog training," he said.

"Maybe I shouldn't have wasted so much time and money on an MBA."

Warren chuckled. "Listen, people shouldn't be manipulated like dogs, but there are similarities in dealing with both. Your job is to find what motivates your team and play off that."

"Motivating Kevin to be tactful—now there's a challenge."

"But not impossible," Warren continued. "Motivation and discipline should be self-directed, but sometimes we need to nudge people. Once your team is under way, you're just there to keep them focused and move things along when they get stalled."

"But, how do I motivate my team members to work together effectively? Especially when we have so little time?"

"Tight timeframes offer good opportunities to implement change. There's little time to resist or spend too much time settling disputes. You handled Kevin really well this morning. It was important that you gave him that immediate feedback."

"Again, I bring the dog training into the picture," I said. "Dog and employee training are essentially behavior modification, and timely feedback is still critical. Otherwise, both dogs and humans may continue doing the same things wrong, thinking everything is fine."

Warren nodded. "And we also have to remember to reward good behavior. For dogs, food, praise, attention, tone of voice, and playtime are important rewards. These and other forms of rewards also apply to people. When a dog does something right, most people naturally praise the dog, give him a treat, or give him a hug. Yet that same person may forget to acknowledge a team member's accomplishments."

WALKING DEWEY LATER THAT EVENING, I thought about what happened during the day. With everything going on, I hadn't followed up with Alex about the Kevin incident. Alex had copied me on some e-mails, so I knew that he had reserved the training facilities. I called his extension to leave him an encouraging voice mail. To my surprise, he picked up.

"Are you still there?" I asked. "It's almost 10:00."

"I just wanted to catch up. Is everything all right?"

"Everything's fine. I just wanted to leave a message to thank you for setting up the training. I also wanted to follow up on the situation with Kevin."

"He talked to me. Everything's cool. I have only two more chapters to finish. Everything else is ready for review."

"That's excellent news. Now go home. I need you at your best tomorrow."

WE'D BEEN ONSITE FOR ONLY THREE DAYS and already Grace's war room table was strewn with documents.

"How are things going?" I asked her.

"Very well, thank you. Tyler's really nice and easy to deal with. I'll update the project plan again by lunch time."

I wanted to tell her how well she was doing and let her know how proud I was of everything she'd accomplished, but the phone rang and interrupted my thoughts. It was Nate, the master of telling clients what they wanted to hear.

"Hey, Marti," he barked into the phone. "We got a problem over at Octaquad. Jenkins, our project manager, just quit. I need you to get over there to assess the situation and keep the project on track."

"I barely have KFI on track. Can't you send someone else?" I responded feeling frustrated beyond measure. Nate thought I could be in two places at once.

"They asked for you. I'm e-mailing you work plans and status reports even as we speak. I want you there by Friday."

"But what about KFI?"

"You'll manage." I heard a buzz from his end of the line. "I have to take this," he said. "As usual," I muttered to myself.

The KFI project, too, was more than enough. How was I going to manage this new project on top of the one that was already out of control and behind schedule? It was time to delegate. My first thought was to hand off KFI to Grace. Would she be up to the task?

WHEN THE PHONE RANG AT 10:00 THAT NIGHT, I jumped like a startled frog. I had fallen asleep at my desk. Who would be calling me at the office at this hour?

It was Hank. I suddenly remembered I was supposed to be home hours ago.

"Are you coming home sometime tonight?"

"I'm sorry I'm so late. You won't believe this but Nate assigned me to yet another project. I got involved and lost track of the time."

"I was getting worried!" I could sense the frustration in his voice.

"I'm sorry," I responded soothingly. "It should be over soon. I promise I'll be on my way home in five minutes."

"I've heard that one before…"

"I know, I know. I promise."

THE NEXT THING I KNEW, it was time for dog training class again. The dogs were all shaking hands with their noses. The canine world had perfected ass kissing long before corporate America. The big sheepdog and Dewey were even getting along better now that they had worked out their appropriate ranks in the pecking order. The owners were all chatting as Jenna entered the room, and everyone suddenly became still.

"Hi, everyone," Jenna began. "Today we're going to work on the STAY command." She quickly commandeered the leash from Rob and took Winston for a spin around the perimeter of the barn. In a firm, clear voice, she commanded him to SIT and STAY. Then she backed away from him, holding her hand in front of herself like a policeman halting traffic. The obedience-challenged Winston tried to get up immediately, but Jenna put a stop to it instantly with a glare that said, "Don't try it."

Winston reluctantly sat back down and let out a little whimper of protest. Jenna then walked about twenty-five feet from the dog and turned to face him again. She continued to hold up a restraining hand, signaling to the dog that he was still under command to stay. After about fifteen seconds, she called, "COME," and Winston galloped to her in two seconds. "Good come, Winston."

Jenna called on Dewey and me to practice the STAY command in front of the class. Dewey was not exactly getting an "A" in dog obedience yet, but at least he wasn't embarrassing me too much. Some of the other dogs are worse than Dewey, I thought, leading him to the front of the class.

I imitated Jenna's actions as best I could, but Dewey did not stay. My glare apparently wasn't as powerful as Jenna's. As Dewey immediately got up and started trotting toward me, I was mortified. I hollered, "NO", and repeated, "Dewey, SIT," and then "STAY" as loudly as I could. My bellowing voice captured his attention, and I was relieved when he actually sat and looked at me, shaking his floppy ears and waiting for what was to come next. I took a deep breath and held my hand out in front. Then, on the COME command, he came barrelling toward me, nearly knocking me down.

He still needed some work, but at least he was enthusiastic. That's all I really hoped—for him not to totally embarrass me—at least for now. "Good, boy Dewey," I sighed with relief.

Jenna then intervened, praising us both on our demonstration. Jenna had certainly mastered the art of giving positive feedback, far surpassing most managers.

"But what if your dog just won't stay?" asked Sue. She should have known better than to ask, as she became the next *victim*. Sue and Buddy, her rag mop sheepdog with hair masking its face, were front and center before she could protest.

"OK, let's see you and Buddy shows us how to do it," Jenna encouraged.

Sue, summoning her most forceful voice, commanded, "Buddy, sit." To her surprise, the dog sat. She then tried to walk away, but Buddy immediately tried to follow. She looked perplexed and didn't know what to do.

Jenna coached from the sidelines. "Repeat the command with conviction."

"STAY!" Sue commanded with all the conviction she could muster as she held up the restraining traffic cop hand Jenna had modeled. Buddy looked confused at first, but miraculously sat and stayed.

"We need to keep working with our dogs and have confidence that they will do as they are commanded. If we don't believe in them, they'll sense our doubt and do what they want instead of what we tell them. So, be sure to practice every day. Tell your dog to stay often, walk thirty feet, and then command him to COME. Practice makes perfect."

After dog training class, I shared with Jenna the doubts I had about my new assignment. I wondered if my people were really up to the challenge with Grace in charge. And even if they were, was the project beyond reasonable capacity? It was mission impossible in so many ways. It would take even more sleepless nights and lots of caffeine.

Then there was the conflict that had embroiled the group. Was it really resolved? How would Grace handle it if Kevin and Alex were back at each other's throats? It would take something extremely creative to get us out of this morale slump. Or maybe a miracle.

Suddenly I jumped up, my eyes sparkling with excitement as if I'd found the answer to the universe. "*The answer lies in empowerment.*

Remember when you told the class that as a dog behaves better, eventually you can reward him with more freedom? I need to empower my team to create the innovative ideas that will drive success."

Paws for Reflection

*Always give constructive
feedback in private.*

*Address sub-standard performance
promptly and firmly.*

*One firm correction is
worth ten tugs.*

Notes

Paws for Reflection

Inconsistency can lead to discipline and morale problems.

Notes

Chapter 7

Empowerment and Grooming: Unleashing Their Full Potential

Jenna's comment made me think more about delegating the KFI project to Grace. I had been giving her more freedom than Alex or Kevin—she was able to get things done right with minimal supervision. I have always tried to be fair with my team, but some team members required more handholding than others.

"You've got something there. Grace is fantastic. Capable, creative, responsive, pleasant," I said.

Jenna was pacing the room now. Her arms were animated as she talked with her hands. "Let Grace lead the team while you're gone."

"That would work." I was energized by the thought. "Prism hasn't even scratched the surface of Grace's potential. If I want to keep a rising star like Grace, I'll have to give her some room to grow or another organization might be glad to give her the opportunity."

Somehow, I wasn't surprised when Jenna said, "It's time to let go of the leash. Once dogs have mastered the basics of come and heel, you can walk them without leashes. They can be trusted to walk along side you, just like loyal team members. When you have a puppy or an unruly dog, you need a short leash. Same with a new hire. But as they become more capable through training, you let the leash out gradually over time and, when they become competent like Grace, you can provide them with an invisible fence. Just be clear on when and how they need to keep you informed and in what situations they should check with you before making a decision. That clarifies their boundaries. Once you've developed trust and respect, the relationship strengthens. Do you feel you can trust Grace to finish this job without you?"

"Yes," I answered, "but…."

"Either you do or you don't. What doubts do you have?"

"I can't think of any offhand. Only that this is a critical project, and we could lose a client over this."

"Isn't that true of every project you work on?" Jenna questioned.

"Yes, but this is my first project in my new role. My own career and reputation are at stake."

Jenna continued, "Then try this—let go of the leash, but be available for assistance and advice at least initially. Give her some autonomy. You can always step back in if she strays too far off course."

It was quiet for a while as we both pondered the possibilities and pitfalls.

"The others may want to challenge the way she manages the project, of course." Jenna pursed her lips. Her mind was spinning; she was in full gear.

"I have to make it clear to the team that Grace is in charge and that what she says goes. It'll work." I got up slowly, still in deep thought. "I'll let you know how things go."

I gained trust with my team by opening myself up, communicating directly, and being more available to them. Now it was time for me to trust them.

The next day I called Grace into a vacant office. "Is everything all right?" she asked, a concerned look on her face.

"Everything is fine. How do you feel about the project so far?"

"Things are hectic right now, but I'm running some tests on the system, so I have a little breathing room."

"Good. First of all, I want to let you know how proud I am of the progress you've made so far. You've done an excellent job. Tyler is very confident in your ability to meet every deliverable on time."

Grace beamed. "Thank you," she said.

"There is something very important I'd like to ask you. Our project manager at Octaquad just resigned, and Nate assigned me to go onsite to assess the situation. I'm going to be here less and less for the rest of the KFI project, and someone needs to take charge. Would you be willing to manage our project from here on? We can touch base whenever you need anything or have questions. I will be here as much as possible and definitely on the go-live date. Do you feel up to this?"

She grinned. "You bet."

"You've proven time and again that you can perform well and get things done with minimal supervision. I trust you. You've got this."

"Thank you. That means a lot to me."

"I'll inform the team, and then I'll let Tyler know that you will be his contact person until go-live. And, again, I will be available if you have any problems or concerns, questions, or whatever."

We discussed more details and key tasks for Grace to follow up on, emphasizing to check with me on any problems or key decisions. Grace was getting up to leave when I asked, "Grace, do you have a few more minutes?"

"Sure."

"I've been meaning to ask you, where do you see yourself heading in your career?"

"Wow! I've never been asked that before," Grace said, as her face lit up with enthusiasm. "People in this company get so caught up in the frenzy of rolling out projects that we never seem to have time for discussions like this. I'm even used to having my performance review months late."

"It's important to make time for these conversations. What do you want to accomplish long term?"

"I want to get into management. I'm hoping to move into something where I can make a real difference."

"You're making a difference now."

"I appreciate that, but I still feel that my hands have been tied for a long time. Before you took over the team, I couldn't make a move without consulting at least two or three people. Our company's excessive red tape makes it difficult to take initiative."

"How so?"

"Just last week, I needed a browser plug-in for the report viewer. It cost less than $300 and didn't interfere with the infrastructure or implementation. Yet I needed five different signatures to get it approved. I have three so far. This project has nearly a million dollar price tag, so $300 is a drop in the bucket. The time I spent chasing down the required approvers and having them review and sign off has already cost more than the price of the software. If we really want to become the agile and empowered organization we keep hearing about, then processes like this must change."

"I agree. We can work on removing some of these obstacles after this project is complete. In the meantime, if other issues come up that are slowing down the KFI project, I want to know right away. So what would you like to do to further your career?"

"I want to continue working on my MBA. I'm twelve credits into it, but time-consuming projects like this keep getting in the way. I've lost the past year of school because different managers won't sign off on my tuition reimbursement application. I keep getting the same excuse: We're really busy right now, but as soon as things calm down, you can get back into your program."

"Grace, I really want you to succeed here. I will do all I can to help you finish your Master's. As busy as we are, you have to make time for your education. After the smoke from this project clears, we can set up a professional development plan to chart your path forward. Let's see if we can get you started in that direction for the fall."

Unlike Jenna's emphasis on clear communication and consistency, our management team was saying one thing and doing another. Our efforts to keep projects under control were actually impeding our staff's ability to get things done and getting in the way of their empowerment and development.

I HAVE A HABIT OF TRYING TO DO too many things at once. For me multitasking is really not a talent; it's an obsession—an obsession that doesn't allow me to do all tasks well. As I tried to fill my empty gas tank on the way to the Octaquad kick-off, I was simultaneously trying to carry on a conversation with Grace on my phone.

"So what did you say the problem was? You're breaking up."

"The network is down, and we're stuck until it's fixed."

I slid my credit card into the card reader. Apparently upside down—I got an error message. "Can you start planning some of the training presentation on paper while you're waiting?" As I asked this, I realized I had pulled up to the gas tank in the wrong direction and the hose didn't reach my side. I got back into the car and started it up again, pulling into the proper position.

"Good idea. I'll get the team together so we can start a rough outline." Grace was always so responsible and so calm—unlike me. Meanwhile, I was still unsuccessfully trying to fill my tank. This time I had inserted the credit card correctly, but then I pushed the wrong button and got another error message. Still trying to pump gas, I noticed the sign: *No cell phones. Can cause an explosion.*

I really have to slow down and stop doing so many things all at once, I thought as I ended the call. But how can I do that when the project is so far behind and obstacles keep popping up like potholes after a long, hard New England winter?

What a great day this would be at the beach, and here I was running from meeting to meeting and bouncing my attention from phone call to text to emails. My thoughts about the nice day changed abruptly when I noticed a police car with its red light flashing in my rear view mirror. Obediently, I pulled over to the side of the road, hoping he'd continue on, but my heart skipped a beat as he pulled right in behind me. My mind explored the possibilities—was I speeding? I didn't think so. Did I make an illegal turn? No. Turns out my registration had expired. In all the chaos of the past few months, sending in my registration renewal—like a lot of other personal responsibilities— must have fallen through the cracks in my mind.

WHEN I FINALLY ARRIVED HOME THAT NIGHT, Hank and Dewey were cuddled together on the living room rug. I startled them as I came through the door at 11:00. Nevertheless, Dewey trotted over with a tail-wagging hello.

Hank, sleepy–eyed, said, "Wow, I can't believe you're just getting home from the office. You've got to stop working so hard."

"Yeah, this project's a nightmare, but at least things are starting to fall into place."

"That's good news. You've certainly been missing in action around here."

"Sorry I missed dinner again," I added.

"When do the long hours end?"

"Soon, I hope, but Nate keeps broadening the scope of the project, adding new deliverables, and even adding a new project. He's lost all sense of reality—especally in terms of how much work is involved to meet his constantly changing demands."

"Well, sooner or later your deadline will come, whether you have the project done or not."

It was true. Our deadline loomed like a big elephant in the room that no one wanted to acknowledge. *I would be glad to be free of it all and get back to a normal life.* Less stress, time for myself, time to have coffee and read the paper on a Sunday morning—and, most important, time to spend with Dewey and Hank as a family again.

Yes. It was time to get this project wrapped up. That night, Hank and I spent some time planning our next vacation—trusting that would happen soon after the project ended. I was due. I had been working eighty hours a week for the past five weeks, and I looked like it. I had dark circles under my eyes, and I was a walking zombie most days. I straggled home at all hours of the night and slept fitfully as I tossed and turned thinking of little details that needed to be taken care of or, worse yet, problems that could still emerge.

THE NEXT MORNING, THE TEAM COULD SENSE my anxiety and was following my lead, becoming more stressed as pressure to perform mounted. I feared we were approaching meltdown. All I could think was I needed some fresh air.

The hot breeze felt like a knife in my chest when I stepped outside to get some fresh air, but fresh air was not to be found. Treading the parking lot felt like walking across the desert at high noon. The asphalt was so hot I thought the soles of my shoes would melt and glue my feet to the pavement. No stress relief outside. I decided that my team and I needed a lift. That's when I borrowed a trick from Jenna and rewarded my team with people treats. That afternoon I brought back ice cream sundaes for everyone. The gesture of appreciation and the short break was not only appreciated but also boosted morale at a difficult time.

That same day, I made it a point to get home at a decent hour and spend time with Hank and Dewey. Together, we practiced Dewey's obedience training, and Hank was impressed with how he had progressed from the little furry couch-eating monster to an attentive and mostly obedient pup in just over a month.

Obedience training had helped Dewey in so many ways. Not only was he becoming woman's best friend, he had calmed down a lot. Dewey would probably never become a canine star, but at least he stopped chewing the furniture. He also gave up jumping on people, knocking them down, and making them instant prisoners. And those were very good changes.

Paws for Reflection

Empowerment enables the freedom to think creatively.

Remove obstacles to empowerment.

Notes

Chapter 8

Accountability: Leading the Pack

I was playing fetch with Dewey in the park early Saturday morning as a short respite before getting back to work. I was tossing his special toy, which he chased and returned to me. Dewey would never willingly stop this activity. In fact, doing this all day would be Dewey's doggie nirvana. I had just flung the toy into a high spinning arc, when I saw a thirty-something man in sweats and a baseball cap pitching a past-its-prime tennis ball to a golden retriever. They were playing fetch, or at least trying to. The dog caught the ball in his mouth after the first bounce and shot back to his owner. The man tried to wrestle the ball from the dog's mouth as it thrashed its head playfully, not letting go, dashing in circles.

"DROP!" He repeated. "DROP!" He managed to tug the ball from his dog's mouth as he saw me approach.

Nodding a quick hello, he inquired, "I saw you playing fetch. How did you get your dog to do that?"

"Do what, play fetch?"

"Sort of, but I actually mean drop the ball," he clarified.

"It wasn't easy, but the dog should drop the toy at your feet before you praise him. Don't accept less or tug of war is all you'll ever get. Do you mind if I try?"

"Sure. What do I have to lose?" He handed over the dog's ball with a skeptical look.

"What's your dog's name?"

"Rocky."

"Do you mind if I give him a treat when he returns? It not only rewards him but distracts him from the ball and gets him to drop it."

He nodded in consent.

I threw the ball as the dog catapulted in its direction. He snapped the ball in mid-air and came barreling back. I didn't try to take the ball from him, but waited until his excitement waned a bit. Then I said, "Rocky, DROP."

The dog continued to dash in circles, but I ignored him and asked his owner to do the same. It took several minutes and a good measure of patience, but eventually he calmed down and dropped the ball. "Good boy, Rocky!" I said enthusiastically as I gave him the treat. The dog was exuberant as he gobbled down the treat and anticipated another throw with the possibility of another treat.

His owner tried it, but it took even longer for the dog to calm down. He was more used to the tug-of-war routine with his owner. But, eventually, Rocky realized that he wasn't going to get tug-of-war; instead, he was only getting ignored. He tried rubbing against his owner's leg to get attention, but when that didn't work, he dropped the ball.

At that point we both exclaimed, "Good boy, Rocky!"

The retriever jumped for joy and waited in anticipation of the next volley.

"That's terrific. How did your dog learn that?"

"He's been going to obedience classes to improve his behavioral problems."

"Well, you'd never know it. He looks like a perfectly behaved dog to me."

"Hardly," I laughed, as a flash of chewed couch drifted through my mind.

We talked for a little while as he practiced his dog's new skill. Occasionally he would be tempted to go back to old behaviors and started to lunge at Rocky to grab the ball. A slight movement of my head from side to side was all he needed to get him back on track.

I explained, "He's playing a different game because he doesn't understand the rules. Define the rules for him, and then hold him accountable. Reward the behavior you want and scold or ignore him when he doesn't do what you want."

MENTALLY, I WAS BACK IN CLASS WITH JENNA. Accountability, she had stressed, goes both ways. You must be accountable to the dog and to those you lead by first setting a good example and abiding by your own standards.

"Accountability goes hand in hand with consistency," Jenna had reminded us. "Be consistent about what you expect and hold your dog accountable for good behavior."

I remember Susan had asked. "But how do you hold a dog accountable?"

"You provide rewards for good behavior and provide bad consequences, like ignoring or scolding the dog, when he does the wrong thing," Jenna had replied.

Jenna had demonstrated the knee to chest technique for getting dogs to stop jumping on people. She started with Winston, the jump-happy rottweiler. After Dewey saw the technique used on Winston, you wouldn't think he'd fall for the bait, but you would be wrong. When Jenna brought Dewey up in front of the class, he predictably jumped on her with his front paws on her waist. She had immediately given him a knee right in the chest, and he sank like a wet dishrag to the floor. As soon as he sat down, Jenna patted him on the head and complimented him. "Good boy. Good boy." In two seconds, she had taught him not to jump up on her by showing him the serious consequences. Hopefully, it was a lesson he would remember forever, but time would tell.

ON MY WAY TO OCTAQUAD, a call from Nate diverted me to the home office for a "very important meeting." The issue was so important, he had stressed, yet I had to wait ten minutes outside his office before he hung up the phone and called me in.

"Marti, HR just called, and they want us to do a post-implementation review on the KFI project for your staff's performance reviews."

By *us*, he meant me.

"You called me in from a client site with a tight project deadline so you could discuss performance reviews? Couldn't this wait?"

In Nate's world, nothing he wanted could wait. He ignored my questions. "I want them rated on the following criteria: Adherence to company standards, maintaining exceptional levels of quality, meeting deadlines, and collaboration."

"When are these due?"

"Next week."

"Shouldn't we wait until the project is finished before we do a post-implementation review?"

"I want them ready for the next executive leadership team meeting."

"Nate, let me get this straight. You want me to rate my team's performance on criteria that we never shared with them? Things that they were never told when we launched the project? That's unfair."

"You make it sound so awful. It's not like that. We call it the contribution rating system. I've been on a cross-functional team with HR, and we think your team at KFI would be a great proof-of-concept case. It helps people find their strengths, identify areas for growth, and weed out the dead wood."

I had heard about the new employee performance review system initiative. This effort was months behind schedule, and HR was eager to launch it before the end of the quarter. "Nate, I think performance reviews are an important part of employee development, but don't you agree that it's unfair to rate their performance based on criteria they knew nothing about beforehand?"

"It's about accountability. You know, getting folks to take responsibility for their actions or lack of action."

"How can we hold people accountable for things that they didn't know they were responsible for?"

"Look, if things don't go well with your little project, somebody has to go. We need a formal process to make it official. Simple as that. You can't just go around firing people for no reason."

I felt like giving Nate a knee to the chest with a resounding "NO!" as Jenna would do with an unruly dog. The discussion with him was like a tug-of-war with a bull dog. We tell the employees the rules when the game is almost over and then are surprised that they were playing a different game all along? We expect top performance without setting clear expectations? We make very general requests then expect highly specific results? Then, when we don't get the outcome we expected, we blame it on employee incompetence. So we fire them (or get rid of the dog that hasn't been taught what is expected).

To hold our employees accountable, we need to show them what good performance looks like.

I WAS ALREADY TEN MINUTES LATE when I caught up with Alex for our status meeting.

I was impressed—he was organized and even slightly ahead of where he was supposed to be on the work plan. "Things look like they're on track. Do you need anything?" I asked.

"I'm good. Thanks. My class materials are ready," he said, "but I thought I'd have more time."

"Why is that?"

"The end-to-end testing period is really short this time. It usually takes a couple of weeks for a company this size, but the latest work plan only shows four days. I've never seen one this brief."

After the meeting, I reviewed the work plan. I knew the timeline had been compressed, but I assumed that Kevin and the KFI project team members would just work longer hours to complete the testing. Comparing it to the previous version of the work plan, I saw that the Advanced Accounting testing had been deleted. Nate sold KFI this additional module in the eleventh hour, but there was no test plan for it.

I immediately surmised where the problem was. Kevin strikes again!

After the first time I coached Kevin, I learned I couldn't just wave my wand and make people do what I wanted. It was difficult to manage people, but it was a lot easier if I spoke straight from the heart. I had to be brutally honest, not only with my team members but also with myself. What was really bothering me? Were they being obstinate toward taking direction or feedback? In Kevin's case, what bothered me most was that he was not being honest and straightforward with me. He wasn't even sharing information I should know about as his manager.

I went to Kevin immediately. He was hunched over his laptop, typing at a furious pace, but coming to a halt as I approached.

"Kevin, I want to talk with you about the test plan. Why aren't you testing Advanced Accounting?"

"Advanced Accounting is a very stable component, it usually doesn't break—"

I interrupted, "Testing is always part of our implementation process. It gives us the one last chance for troubleshooting before our go-live date. You know that."

Looking down at his twiddling fingers, he said nothing.

"Kevin, you've violated our procedures," I began. "You can't just eliminate a significant part of the work plan without consulting me or at least someone else on the team."

"I was only trying to save us time."

"Yes, but we have procedures for a reason."

"Sometimes, you've got to cut corners when you're under a tight deadline." He put his hands on his hips as he dug in his heels. "Besides, Nate told me to do whatever it takes—and that's what I did."

"Sounds like Nate." I pursed my lips, shaking my head in frustration. "But even if Nate did order you to do it, you should have let me know about it. I need to be in the loop."

Kevin just kept repeating that he was merely following orders as he stared at the barren desk in front of him.

I closed my eyes in frustration. I could hear horns honking, as rush hour was in full swing. A siren blared in the distance. *Another late night at the office,* I lamented to myself.

"Kevin, think of the consequences of what you did. Instead of saving time, we now have to retest the entire program to accommodate Advanced Accounting. It could take days longer than the original plan."

I took a deep breath and counted to ten in my head, sparing Kevin from a throttling. I'd had more than enough of Kevin's cockiness. Today, he had taken it to a new level.

"I knew I shouldn't have taken that shortcut even as Nate ordered me to do it."

I just nodded. "Kevin—"

"Marti, please let me finish. You know, even a couple of weeks ago I would have passed the buck on this to Nate or blamed the whole problem on you or whoever was convenient. But it was really just me. It's my fault. I should just quit. I appreciate what you've done. I should have just told Nate what he wanted to hear, then done the right thing."

"Kevin—" I paused a moment. Who is this guy, and what has he done with my obnoxious Kevin? He looks and sounds like Kevin but he's making sense. Whoever he is, I think I like him better. Here I was reprimanding Kevin again—the seventh time in six weeks. But this time was different. We had hit a turning point. "I think you can still do the right thing."

He just looked at me stunned, running his fingers through his thinning pate. "If we do things the right way, we'll never deliver on time," he lamented.

"We'll find a way. How far are we into testing the other components?"

"Only two days."

Testing was slightly behind schedule, but in this case we weren't so far into it that we couldn't include Advanced Accounting in the next phase. I said gently, "Let me talk to Tyler. He'll be reasonable. It may take even longer hours, a weekend, and gallons of Starbucks, but we can still make it."

Kevin nodded hesitantly, his face slowly transforming from a nervous smile to a confident, but not cocky, grin.

I had convinced Kevin. Now all I had to do was convince myself.

The meeting with Tyler went well. He arranged for three of his staff to work through the weekend offering them comp time later in the year. A phone call to Warren got us an additional tester from his team. But with the modified testing schedule, it would still delay implementation by two weeks.

"I don't think that will be an issue," Tyler said.

"But, Tyler, we don't want to deliver it late."

"Marti, I think we can get what we need for now from the basic version of the Omega Suite. I know the original plan calls for the advanced version, but it would be easier to map Advanced Accounting to the basic version and upgrade the system to the advanced version next year."

"Great idea! That would give us time to fully test everything else with a little padding to spare," I said. "But I need to contact Nate to make sure this agrees with the sales contract and service level agreement." I immediately left Nate a voice mail.

ONCE AGAIN I RALLIED THE TROOPS. "Even though we are now only installing Omega Basic, we still have our work cut out for us. Due to the additional Advanced Accounting module testing, I need all the help I can get. Even those of you who aren't techies can test for usability. This will take us through the weekend. I apologize for the inconvenience, but this project absolutely needs to not only succeed, but must also be delivered on time."

After the meeting, Kevin called me aside. "Where can I reach you if there's a problem over the weekend?"

"Just come get me. I'll be in the war room helping you test software."

"Really?" He seemed amazed.

"What? You think I would load you guys down with work, and then dash off to the beach for the weekend?"

"That's what Nate would do. We'll be glad to have you."

I tried to call Nate for a quick update, but he had gone for the day.

IT WAS DEWEY-TRAINING NIGHT AGAIN. As I relayed my tale about my conversation with Kevin to Jenna, it became clear to me like the bright stars on a clear, cold January night. "You know, Jenna, I've learned that honesty builds trust and, even though the information may not be pleasant, if it comes from your heart, it helps build a connection; the kind that solidifies a relationship."

"Honest, constructive feedback demonstrates that you are willing to go out of the comfort zone and step over the edge. You're instigating a moment of discomfort in order to lay the foundation of that relationship and to help the individual improve," Jenna added.

"In this case, the feedback not only helped Kevin improve his work performance, but also helped him develop better relationships. It's been rewarding to see him become more accepted. He'll be a better person in the end." I realized I was partially comforting myself, still feeling the sting of our conversation.

We were both deep in thought and didn't speak for a minute.

Kevin had been offensive, I thought, and I couldn't stand his arrogance. Yet when we had our heart-to-heart discourse, I noted that his wall of superiority had chipped away a little. Criticism didn't dishearten him, and he took it fairly well. Maybe people didn't often give him honest feedback, at least in a constructive way. I'm sure he would ponder my words over the next several days and hopefully find a way to instill some understanding and empathy in his daily interactions with others.

"Kevin's abrasiveness is far from gone," I continued. "It'll take more than one coaching session to turn him around—like melting an iceberg, a few drops at a time."

Jenna nodded. "Coaching is an ongoing process. It's not like one-stop shopping. I've been working with my dog trainer, Gary, on his customer relations. He's really good with dogs, but when it comes to people, he doesn't seem to have much sense."

I emphasized further. "Perseverance is what it takes. A baby step every time you work with your team members."

"But when you start to see little improvements, this makes it all worthwhile," Jenna summarized.

We both said, "Amen," as we bade farewell until the next dog training class.

THE NEXT DAY, NATE STILL HADN'T RESPONDED to my texts. And, once again, I left him another one and called to leave a voice message as well.

I stopped in at the office around lunchtime to pick up a copy of the new signed contract with KFI. I asked Nate's admin where he was. She told me he was at an important offsite meeting and that I could leave a message.

On the way out, I saw Nate emerge from his Merccdes in a golf shirt and crisp linen khakis, phone in hand, chatting incessantly in full suck-up mode. There was no doubt where the offsite "meeting" had been. I waited for him at the door, making eye contact as he passed. He stopped outside the door, but his phone conversation continued another two minutes before he asked the caller if he could excuse himself for a moment. Muting the phone, he turned to me and said, "I'm on with Hamilton the veep. This'll be a while. Can I call you when I'm done?" It wasn't really a question. Greg Hamilton, vice president of HR, had the sense of humor of an IRS auditor.

How could Nate expect to have credibility and trust when he couldn't even return a simple phone call? I had decisions to make, and I couldn't count on Nate, so I called Warren and explained my situation. "He expects everything the minute he asks for it, then moves on to something else, often forgetting what he asked for in the first place. I've met toddlers with longer attention spans," I complained. I could feel my blood pressure surging upwards as I spoke.

"Marti, Nate has been a star salesperson, pulling in a lot of money for a long time. When an arrogant prima donna brings in the bucks, the suits often look the other way. But his *modus operandi and Midas Touch* have been wearing off a bit lately, and when the cash flow dwindles, obnoxious behavior becomes less tolerable. I nodded as Warren continued. "The way you describe it, he's the first one to take a bow and a bonus if all goes well, but when the doggie-doo hits the fan, he's only too glad to shift the blame."

"Well, as the dog trainer said, accountability cuts both ways. If you only take the praise, then you're only taking partial accountability. You've got to take the bad with the good."

WARREN CONFIDED, "NATE'S INITIAL SALES SUCCESS made him feel entitled to push his subordinates around. But his 'whatever it takes to get it done' is no longer working. There've been quality issues with software after installation because he forced people to rush through implementations."

"I can vouch for that first hand."

"I've been on the HR Performance rating team with him, too. It could be an effective peer review system, but the company is using it as a tool to push out people it doesn't want around anymore. If I were Nate, I'd watch my back."

When I got off the phone, I saw Kevin standing in front of Grace and Alex at the other end of the war room, hands waving like a conductor. Something was up, but what?

It didn't take long to find out. As I listened to the banter, I could hear references to Nate's indiscretions. What had he done to cause such a stir? Just then, Kevin noticed my quizzical look. "Well you obviously don't know the latest," Kevin exclaimed. *He's getting better,*

I thought, *but he's still the office gossip*. Old habits die hard. Regardless of my resistance to office gossiping, my ears perked up as he waved me over. I felt flattered that he was including me.

"Did you hear? Hamilton called Nate in from the golf course. He wanted to see Nate right away." Kevin sounded like a gloating little boy whose little sister was in trouble instead of him. "All I know is Nate was making promises we couldn't keep. There's talk of clients suing us."

No wonder Nate hadn't responded. Suddenly, saving the KFI account took a back seat to saving himself.

My phone rang. The ID read *Hamilton, Greg*.

Uh Oh, I thought. *Is my head on the chopping block, too?*

Greg told me Nate had been "optimized." This was HR speak for fired. The actual reason would never be made public, but by the end of the day, we would get an official e-mail wishing Nate the best of luck in his future endeavors. For the time being, I was allowed to renegotiate the terms of our service level agreement with KFI.

It wasn't the best weekend of my life, but at least it was a rainy Saturday. Working through a foul-weather weekend isn't quite as frustrating.

The war room had almost a festive atmosphere. I could smell the sweet aroma of oranges in the coffee room as Kevin helped Grace prepare a treat for coffee break. He scampered about pouring coffee and tea into large mugs for everyone and arranged orange slices around a plate of coffee cake squares. People were in shorts, and my team wore polo shirts with the colorful Prism logo.

Everyone was laughing. Funny how food can help brighten up a dreary day. It was especially rewarding to see Kevin finally mesh into the group.

The moment he saw me, Kevin darted over, clipboard in hand, looking more like a camp director than a Software Quality Control Analyst. "So far, we've found only eleven bugs, all of them fixable. Tyler's folks did a great job of cleansing the data before the import. It's so much easier to work with them compared to the past few projects."

Hearing a positive, complaint-free report from Kevin was a rare gift, even if he mentioned some bugs in the software. I walked down the hall to a large meeting space that Alex had transformed into a software classroom. "How's everything going here?"

"Good. I'm just making sure everything is properly installed, so my students won't waste class time troubleshooting." Even a couple of weeks ago, I would have questioned his preparedness, but he had matters under control and was leaving nothing to chance.

Even though Grace was at a temporary workstation, she had managed to clutter her table with defect reports as she plugged away at her keyboard.

Operations were looking good for Monday's go-live.

Several hours later, as I was looking out the window watching the rain clear up, Tyler approached me. "Is something wrong?" I asked.

He quipped. "You won't believe this."

"What?" I braced myself for the latest catastrophe.

"We sailed through testing. We're up and running."

Paws for Reflection

Motivation is driven by anticipated rewards, consequences, and the probability that they will occur.

Reminder: Clarify expectations for optimal performance

Notes

Chapter 9

You *Can* Teach an Old Dog New Tricks

I met Jenna for coffee at Spike's. We'd been through a lot since we first met each other there just a few months ago.

"I have something for you," she said, handing me a large, flat envelope. I gently slid out an eight-by-ten photograph of Dewey in a graduation cap.

"It only took one biscuit to get him to keep the hat in place," I reminded Jenna. The graduation had gone well. Although there were no valedictorian speeches, and the dogs didn't throw their caps in the air, the graduates proved they could successfully sit, stay, and heel. One could tell from the speed of the tails wagging, they all had a doggone good time.

Jenna asked me about work.

"The KFI project is up and running. And we're gearing up for a much larger implementation for a new client."

Jenna grinned. "Marvelous."

"I still don't know how we managed to get this project-from-hell to completion on time, but at this point it feels like heaven."

"Now that the bruises have started to heal, you can take a well-deserved rest."

"I certainly plan to. You know, I'm amazed at how well the principles I've learned from your class aligned with our project."

Jenna paused, taking a sip from her cappuccino, and asked, "If you had to list the top three things you learned from this experience, what would they be?"

I considered her question for a moment. "There are so many, but I would have to say that the top three include setting clear expectations, giving timely feedback, and accountability addressing swift consequences to improve performance."

"Tell me more," Jenna said.

"The dog training gave me a whole new perspective. It's amazing how much people—and all living creatures—need to clearly understand what is expected of them. Otherwise they make mistakes trying to figure things out. It was really obvious to me when dogs did not 'get it' in your training class, but I wasn't aware of how much I had unintentionally confused my team. By learning to set clear expectations, I helped them understand what we needed to achieve and to make sure they were headed in the right direction. Prompt feedback lets them know that what they're doing is right or wrong. And employees need to understand both the good and bad consequences of their actions." I continued. "The three together create a process of continuous performance improvement: Creating clear direction, rewarding positive behavior, and providing corrective guidance when necessary."

"It all comes down to clarity. It's the foundation of my training. There's nothing really difficult about it," Jenna noted.

"If it's so simple, why don't more managers do it?"

"Excellent question," she said.

"Sometimes, when we get so caught up in these incredibly complex and fast-paced projects, we overlook the obvious."

Epilogue

Lessons sometimes come from the most unusual places.

I felt strange moving into Nate's old office. But Grace would need mine. Octaquad was going to need our help, and we were putting together another team for the next project.

Kevin stuck his head in the door. "Good morning, Marti. How was the beach this weekend?"

"Autumn is my favorite time of year at the beach. The weather is still wonderful and the crowds are gone."

"Nothing wrong with that."

I asked about his family. "How's Louise? And Tim?"

"She's still adapting to the empty nest. And Tim actually called last night. He claims to be keeping up with his homework. It's funny, but I actually miss that noise he called music coming from his room. It's eerily quiet without him."

"How are things with Octaquad?"

"Grace and I will have a work plan to you by end of day tomorrow."

"Looking forward to it. Have a great one."

"You, too," he said ducking out. Then he turned around and came back in. "Marti, I almost forgot to tell you. I saw Nate in the park on Saturday."

"Oh, really?"

"Yeah, he was walking this big dog. Well, trying to walk the dog. It was running all over the place, barking up a storm, trying to jump on people. The leash got so tangled around his shins that he tripped and fell. Boy, were his jeans muddy."

For once, it looked like Nate hadn't landed on his feet.

I had a hard time picturing Nate in jeans. Or even dirty. But I had no problem seeing him ignore what wasn't working and still not learning. This made me think of Hank's favorite quote from a philosophy professor: "One of the first signs of maturity is the realization of how much we don't know, how much we still have to learn, and how much we can learn from others."

Our teachers can be older or younger, they don't have to be more experienced, and they don't even have to be human.

Summary of Principles

Communication: They Have to Know What You Expect

Unclear expectations lead to confusion, frustration, insecurity, and mistakes.

Honest Communication builds the foundation for trust

Communicate your expectations clearly. Guide them in the right direction.

Building a Sound Relationship: They've Got to Know You're Trustworthy

Honest communication builds the foundation for trust.

Earn their trust and loyalty will follow.

Without trust you can't build a positive, long-lasting relationship.

Leadership: Be a Master First, a Friend Second

Earn their respect. Lead by your actions.

Establish yourself as top dog: Be the leader of the pack.

Feedback, Rewards and Motivation: We're all Motivated by a Pat on the Head

Use sincere praise as a motivator.

Reinforce your expectations. Provide constructive, timely feedback.

Constructive feedback improves performance and it doesn't cost a dime.

Connect a reward with a specific behavior.

Discipline and Consequences: Four Paws Up or In the Doghouse Again

Always give constructive feedback in private.

Address sub-standard performance promptly and firmly.

One firm correction is worth 10 tugs,

Inconsistency can lead to discipline and morale problems.

Empowerment and Grooming: Unleashing Their Full Potential

Empowerment enables the freedom to think creatively.

Remove obstacles to empowerment.

Accountability: Leading the Pack

Motivation is driven by anticipated rewards, consequences, and the probability that they will occur.

Reminder: Clarify expectations for optimal performance.

Hold yourself accountable first. Lead by example.

Accountability increases personal credibility and improves morale and performance.

You Can Teach an Old Dog New Tricks

Learn by looking at the same problem from a different perspective.

About the Authors

Diane Hanson

Photo by Brenda Schrier Photography

Diane Hanson has helped many organizations develop highly functioning teams and competent and caring managers. Her wide variety of experience includes work with private industry such as pharmaceutical and financial companies, as well as universities, local, state and federal governments and non-profits.

Diane was owner of Creative Resource Development, Inc. for 28 years. Prior to starting her own business, she was an award-winning sales manager with Ayerst Laboratories (now Pfizer Pharmaceuticals) and has worked as a contract training manager at Astra Zeneca.

Under her leadership as Mayor of Dewey Beach, Delaware, for six years, the town is now a beautiful family-friendly beach community that swells from 300 residents to up to 40,000 in summer. Dewey Beach also became one of the most dog-friendly beach towns on the East Coast during her tenure with dog-friendly hotels, rentals and some restaurants. There are many dog events throughout the year including two greyhound weekends, doodle weekend, golden retriever weekend, and Chihuahua races for Cinco de Mayo.

Diane has always had a love of animals and served as Chairman of the Board of Directors for the Chester County SPCA (now Brandywine SPCA) for three years.

After receiving her BS degree from Cornell University, Diane graduated with distinction from the University of Pennsylvania with her MS in Organizational Dynamics.

Todd Cameron

 Todd Cameron is a Technical Product Leader for a corporate innovation lab. Collaborating with large multinational corporate clients, he leads emerging technology early-stage incubation projects. He has more than 20 years of software industry experience, specializing in Blockchain, scrum, Lean Startup, and reporting analytics applications. A frequent presenter on tax and technology topics, he belongs to the Scrum Alliance and Accounting Blockchain Coalition. He holds a Bachelor's Degree from Temple University and a Master's from Penn State. He lives with his family outside of Philadelphia.

Discussion Guide for
Management Unleashed:
Leadership Lessons from my Dog

This group discussion guide includes questions for enhancing book club discussions, study group conversations, life coaching and for anyone who would like to delve more deeply into the content of this book. The suggested questions will help your group find unique and interesting topics for your discussion, enhance your enjoyment of the book, and improve your ability to apply its principles. *For more information, see http://managementunleashed.com.*

BACKGROUND INFORMATION

In the book the main character, Marti, is a young manager learning to lead her team effectively in today's fast-paced and rapidly-changing environment. Partly autobiographical and partly fiction, this fable provides insights to help you better understand behavior.

Throughout their leadership careers, the authors frequently marveled at similarities in motivation and performance outcomes based on analagous techniques with team members, children and dogs. After all, we share common motivators: praise, attention, rewards and caring relationships.

A quick read with lasting, immediately-applicable insights, you'll find yourself recognizing behaviors in your employees, children, and pets. These principles will enable you to deal effectively with professional and personal situations.

TOPICS & QUESTIONS FOR DISCUSSION

The following questions will help you get discussion flowing and increase everyone's learning.

Overall questions about the Book:

1. What is the significance of the title? How does it relate to the contents of the book? What other title might you choose?

2. Why do you think the authors chose to tell this story?

3. Did the book capture the environment of today's fast-paced work world? How?

Characters:

4. Did any of the characters remind you of yourself or someone you know? How?

5. Which characters in the book did you like best? Which characters did you like least? Would you want one of these characters on your team? Why or why not?

6. Were there any moments where you disagreed with the choices or actions of any of the characters? What would you have done differently?

7. Did you think the ending was appropriate? How would you have liked to have seen the book end?

Learnings or Insights Gained from the Book:

8. What scene resonated most with you personally in either a positive or negative way? Why?

9. What similarities in behavior do you see with pets and people in general?

10. How might your new insights from the book help in your daily activities as a manager, leader, parent, or counselor?

11. Share a favorite quote or principle from the book. Why did this quote or principle stand out for you?

12. How does the analogy of a short leash for a puppy or new employee, and an invisible fence for a more experienced employee, apply to empowerment of individuals—whether they are team members or family members?

13. In Chapter Two, the following principle is introduced: "Unclear expectations lead to confusion, frustration, insecurity, and mistakes." Give an example of how this applies to your work or life in general.

14. Without trust you can't build a positive, long-lasting relationship. Do you believe this principle to be true and why?

15. When is it important to establish yourself as "Top Dog?" When is it NOT appropriate?

16. "Constructive feedback improves performance and it doesn't cost a dime." So why isn't it used more?

17. "Always give constructive feedback in private." Relate an experience relevant to this principle.

18. "Address sub-standard performance promptly and firmly. One firm correction is worth 10 tugs." Do you agree? If so, how does this principle apply to employees, children and people in general?

19. How can "inconsistency lead to discipline and morale problems?"

20. "Motivation is driven by anticipated rewards, consequences, and the probability that they will occur." Do you agree? How does this relate to dogs, kids, and employees?

21. "Hold yourself accountable first. Lead by example." Give an example of how Marti holds herself accountable and leads by example.

22. How can you remove obstacles to empowerment?

23. Are there additional principles the authors should have included?

24. Which principle would you like to work on to improve your effectiveness? How do you plan to incorporate it into your everyday life?

In memoriam to Bogie,
a wonderful dog.

May he rest in peace.
2009–2018

46640054R00076

Made in the USA
Columbia, SC
30 December 2018